A Kid in the Fifties

LIFE IN AN OREGON LUMBER TOWN

JOHN LEARD

Fulton Books, Inc.
Meadville, PA

Published by Fulton Books 2021

ISBN 978-1-63710-672-3 (paperback)
ISBN 978-1-63710-673-0 (digital)

Printed in the United States of America

Preface (and Disclaimer)

To my kids (since all they know about my childhood is a bit here and a piece there):

I wrote this for fun, so read it that way. I know there are dangling marsupials, mixed tenses, and propositions...which I ended sentences with. But since I don't know my tense from my tepees, just ignore them. I do hereby swear (don't tell the grandkids) that the following facts are true to the best of my recollection. However, my photographic memory has been out of film for years, so just take my word for it. What few people mentioned that still survive probably don't remember anything, either, so lots o' luck trying to verify anything I say.

Luv ya! Enjoy!

My family (also known as "the Rogues Gallery")!

Dad

His name was John Isaac Leard but was known to most as Ike, probably to save confusion with his dad, also John. He was born in Lindale, Texas, about halfway between Dallas and Shreveport, Louisiana, on April 2, 1905. He was an only child, was born in the later years of his parents' lives, and grew up working on his parents' dairy farm. (He used to say if he ever milked another cow, it'd be too soon!) He spent his adult life in many parts of Texas, working for others as a farmer, until moving to Oregon in 1951. There, he worked at Santiam Lumber Co., a mill in Sweet Home, until retirement. His main pastime was fishing but learned to love deer and elk hunting after we moved to Oregon.

Dad was the main disciplinarian of the family. Mom was usually the one deferring the punishment by saying, "Just wait 'til your daddy gets home!" Dad had a strap hanging on the bathroom wall that was a barber's "razor strop" (no, that's not a misprint) for sharpening straight razors back when they still used them. It was actually two leather straps, one on top of the other, so when it hit your rear, it was kind of like "whap...whap!" Two for the price of one, so to speak. He would hold onto one of your hands, so you ran around in circles, trying to outrun that strap. Superman might be faster than a speeding bullet, but I swear he'd never have outrun that strap! Dad spanked our bottoms but never hit us otherwise. He always said the Good Lord made only one spot for spanking or, as they called it back then, a whippin'. Dad passed on in a nursing home in Sweet Home on January 6, 1994. He was almost eighty-nine years old.

Mom

Mintoria Leard, no middle name, was born on October 29, 1909, in Dennison, Texas, north of Dallas, close to the Oklahoma border. She said her first name was of Indian origin (Native American, not the Eastern kind) but was taken from an aunt by the same name.

She was from a family of twelve children, six by her mom and six more by her stepmom. As far as I know, all of them except one lived in Texas. Uncle Roy, her next youngest brother, settled in Oregon after his hitch in the Navy.

Mom was four feet, eleven inches at her peak and late in life, only weighed about 110 pounds. (Her nickname was "Midge," which I used to think was due to her size, but later on, I learned that a "midge" is also a pesky bug, so then I wondered if her brothers had the other definition in mind.) She married Dad on October 14, 1928, and gave birth to nine kids over twenty-three years. She was a feisty one for her size, and once, when Wayne ran from her to avoid a whippin', she picked up a piece of well rope and threw it at him. It "lassoed" his legs, so he fell on his face, and all she had to do was walk up and use the rope on his backside! Discipline was a lot different in those days, but not one of us suffered any physical effects as a result. And we all knew if Mom gave us a spanking, it was really a last resort—we must have really deserved it. Mom passed on at Willamette Manor in Lebanon, Oregon, on December 20, 2007, at ninety-eight years of age.

Gladys Nell

The first of the bunch, she was born on October 14, 1929, in Wellington, Texas, in the panhandle east of Amarillo. Her brothers used to make her cry by telling kids at school she was born on the day our folks got married, not bothering to mention it was exactly one year later! Since she was seventeen years older than I and Mom had other things to take up her time, she kind of raised me for the first few years, and for much longer, she tried to treat me like I was her own. She married Buford Justice in her late teens, but he left her before their son David was born. She remarried Charlie Shreffler, and after he finished his four years in the Air Force, she moved with him back to his hometown of Barnsdall, Oklahoma. They had another son Chuck and a daughter Pam.

Gladys passed away in Barnsdall, Oklahoma, on September 12, 2017.

William Newton (Bill)

Bill was also born in Wellington, Texas, on July 10, 1931. He skipped two grades in school, so he graduated the same year as Gladys. He had the grades, but he was only sixteen, so colleges didn't want him back then, plus they cost money, which the folks didn't have. He joined the Navy in 1949, wound up in the medical corps, and was sent to Korea. He was assigned to the Marines since they didn't have any corpsmen. He stayed in the Navy until 1974, bouncing back and forth between the Naval hospitals in San Diego and the east coast, as well as serving two tours in Vietnam. Bill married Jo (Josephine) Smith, and they had four girls, Elaine, Annette, and twins, Beverly and Brenda. After the Navy, Bill worked as a San Diego County deputy coroner until retirement. Bill passed on at his home in El Cajon, California, on July 18, 2003.

James Dee (Jim)

Jim was the third child born in Wellington, Texas, on April 19, 1933. I heard that the middle name was originally just the initial "D," but the folks got tired of explaining that he had no middle name, so they added the double E to avoid confusion. He graduated from high school the month our family moved to Oregon. Just before or just after the Army, he went back east to Pennsylvania with a buddy, and I was told he pitched minor league baseball for a while. He served in the Army from 1953 to 1956, including one tour in Korea. He married Jean Alexy, who had a daughter Peggy, then together, they had two more girls, Denny and Cynthia. Jim worked a few years after the Army at Santiam Lumber Mill then moved to a small machine shop in Lebanon called Linn Gear Works, where he retired as general manager.

Jim passed on in Lebanon on March 24, 2005.

Robert Allen (Bob)

Bob was born in Mathis, Texas, on December 17, 1936. Mathis is clear across the state from Wellington, down in the southeast area. I'm not aware of why the family moved that far between '33 and '36, but that's where they were. Bob quit high school before graduation and joined the Army in 1954 at the age of seventeen. In 1956, after one and a half years, he was stationed at Fort Richardson, Anchorage, Alaska, when he got very ill. He was diagnosed with type 1 diabetes and given a medical discharge. After he went to work at Linn County Telephone in Lebanon, he married Shirley Anderson, and they had two girls, Valerie and Juanita. The phone company was a subsidiary of Pacific Power and Light, which Bob continued to work for. He retired in Pendleton, Oregon, where he was the office manager. Bob passed away on August 16, 2014, following a prolonged battle for life following heart bypass surgery.

Kenneth Wayne (Wayne)

Wayne was also born in Mathis, Texas, on November 11, 1938. He was only twelve years old when we moved to Oregon, so he went all his high school years in Lebanon. He excelled in sports and even had his name on the intramural sports trophy there. He always said the coach wanted him on the track team, but he had to work after school at the bowling alley. He graduated from Lebanon Union High School in 1957 and joined the Navy, where he served in various areas of the South Pacific and Japan. He got out of the Navy in 1961 and worked at various jobs around Lebanon then went back into the Navy in 1964, where he served two more years at Pearl Harbor, Hawaii. Upon returning to Lebanon, he married Eunice Swanson, and they had a son Daniel and a daughter Barbara. Wayne started working at Linn Gear Works in Lebanon as a machinist but soon moved on to Northwest Industries in Albany, where he specialized in making parts from all kinds of rare metals for medical, military, and space technologies. He retired as a master machinist. Wayne passed on at his home in Albany on January 8, 2010.

Martha Pauline (Pauline)

Pauline was born on September 26, 1941. At that time, work must have been scarce in Texas because the family was living in Cove, Arkansas, with my grandpa Leard when she was born. She was only nine years old when we moved to Oregon, so most of her school days were in Lebanon. She quit halfway through high school, went to live with Bill and Jo in the east for a year or so, came back to Lebanon, and worked at a nursing home. She later married Alan Stout, and they had three children, Jeff, John, and Lori. Alan was a logger, so they lived in various coastal areas of Oregon and Washington during their marriage. After their divorce, she married Art Osorio, but a few years later, she passed away of a heart attack on November 15, 1987, at age forty-six.

John Edward (Ed)

That would be me. I was born up in the northern part of Texas, in Whitewright, a few miles east of Dennison and not far from the Oklahoma border, on December 7, 1946. As will be seen later in my story, I was only four going on five years old when we moved to Oregon in June 1951, so I don't have much recollection of life in Texas. Okay, maybe a few incidents. One was when there was a tornado heading our way, so Mom and Dad were trying to hustle us all down into the cellar until it passed. Just about every house in the south in those days had a storm/root cellar. It was a storm cellar for the obvious reason but also called a root cellar because that's where they stored vegetables, such as potatoes, for the winter. It was cool and dark, so the veggies would keep longer, but that's exactly why I didn't want to go down there—because it was cold and dark! Dad told me I would either go down there under my own power, or he was going to drag me down there, feet first. You never wanted to find out if Dad was bluffing, so down I went. One of those times in the cellar, Dad found a big snake lying on a shelf behind the jars of canned fruit. That certainly added to the fondness I already had for the place!

On that same note, Mom sent me out with Pauline to gather the eggs one day. Pauline was only about eight or nine, so the nests were up higher than her head. By tiptoeing and reaching, she would feel around in the nest for the eggs. At one nest, as she reached for the eggs, what she got was the slimy body of a chicken snake that had crawled in to eat the eggs. She let out a scream. They probably heard all the way downtown—and we lived out in the country! Well, they told me chicken snakes are nonvenomous, so the only way they are deadly is if you kill yourself running into the chicken housedoor on the way out. I suppose Mom had to take care of the snake and finish gathering the eggs that day.

Along with all those hens my folks kept for the eggs, we also had a big red rooster. I guess I was only about two at the time because that rooster was about as big as I was. It seemed that every time I went outside, that darned thing would run at me. And if that didn't work, he would fly at me, wings flapping and talons stretched forward in an attack mode! When he found that I would run from him, I immediately became his favorite target. It got so that I wouldn't even go outside to play, so the rooster lost his head one day—literally, that is—and must have become part of our dinner.

I don't know where I got it, but when I was only about a year old, I had a baby ring. I, of course, don't remember any of it, but this is what I was told later in life. At some point one day, I showed up in front of Mom without it on my finger. She very sternly asked me what had become of the ring. I either couldn't talk yet or chose not to. Instead, I took her by the hand and led her around to the side of the house, where I had stuck my ring in a crack in the foundation! I've always tried to have a savings account. I guess that was my first deposit.

Another time when I was about to turn four, I had a piggy bank, in which I was saving money to buy a teddy bear. When my aunts and uncles came to visit, I was told very strictly that I was not to ask them to contribute. So being a devious little boy, I managed to bring out that piggy bank during their visit and inform them that I could not ask them for any money! Of course, the idea worked, and they all chipped in. I still have that little black-and-white teddy bear in my souvenirs, except that it has a brown grilled backside now, thanks to my daughter Lisa leaving it on the floor heater grate at the Air Force base housing when she was about six months old.

When we lived in Texas, a lot of the farms had windmills to pump their well water. Whenever a storm came, you had to disengage the windmill from the pump; otherwise, the thing would get going so fast it would damage or sometimes destroy the whole assembly. On one such occasion, it was late in the evening, and Dad asked Bob, who was about thirteen, to go out and disengage the windmill. He didn't want to go out in a storm by himself, so he asked me to go out with him. I, being only about three years old, had no intention of going outside in the dark, so I just told him, "Not me. I'm just as scared as you are!" Well, that didn't set very well with Bob, who had to go on out and do the job alone.

Enough stories from Texas…

I started school in Lebanon in 1953, almost seven years old, due to my December birthday, at Crowfoot Elementary School. During those first six years, they built Seven Oaks Junior High just a couple hundred yards from there, so I got to move there for my seventh and eighth grades. I loved school but had a hard time in those particular schools because both the grade school and junior high were right next door to the White Oaks housing development, or as we called it, "Snob Hill." It was the newest and most expensive place in Lebanon to live, so a lot of my schoolmates were sons or daughters of doctors, lawyers, and wealthy professionals. I was at the top of my class scholastically, so I became well acquainted with many of them, but I felt I could never become very good friends with any of them since my family didn't have the kind of money it took to travel in their circles. There were, however, many kids from my part of town, several of which I went all twelve grades with, so those were the ones that made up my circle of friends.

I was active in journalism in both junior high and high school and was editor of both school newspapers in the eighth and eleventh grades. All through school, I had told everyone that's what I wanted to be, a journalist. But in my senior year, the school started up their very first electronics class using a bunch of old WWII radio gear. That's where my career took a major turn. After graduation in 1965, I was already accepted to Oregon State University and had several college courses completed in high school, but I didn't have any scholarships and no money. So I thought if I could just work a year, I would have the money saved to go back to college. I got a job at Linn Gear Works, where my brother Jim worked, and Wayne and Ray would later work. Although I never got very good as a machinist, I learned a lot about the trade while running a lathe.

But the plan was short-lived. In December of that year, I got my draft notice, and although I had had rheumatic fever in 1955, which damages the heart valves, I passed the induction physical with flying colors! All this occurred right at the hottest part of the Vietnam War, so rather than be sent to Vietnam as a foot soldier, I joined the Air Force. When the recruiter asked me what career field I would prefer, I remembered that electronics course in high school and how the teacher had assured us all that that was where the big money was—in electronics. So off I went after boot camp to Biloxi, Mississippi, and became an airborne radio repair technician. When I was just about done with my four-year hitch, I took an electronics correspondence course to get my FCC license, which I knew was required to work as a technician in the civilian world. After the Air Force, I worked for thirty-two years for Pacific Gas and Electric Company and retired as a telecommunications technician in Sacramento, California. While I was in the military, I married Frances Williams, and we had two children, Lisa Sharon and John Daniel. After twelve years, we were divorced, and I married Sharon Upchurch, who had a son Brian and a daughter Holly.

Donald Glen

Donald was born in Wheeler, Texas, on November 28, 1950, just a few months before our move to Oregon. But he died at birth due to strangulation from the umbilical cord. My dad always blamed the doctor who came to our house to deliver the baby, saying he, the doctor, was too drunk to function properly.

Weldon Ray (Ray)

Ray was born in Lebanon, Oregon, on April 29, 1953, and as far as I know, he was the only child in the family to be born in a hospital. Ray went to the same schools in Lebanon that I did but quit high school to join the Navy in 1970. He got out after eight years and worked at various jobs after that, including being a machinist at, yes, Linn Gear Works! It seemed to be the logical place to learn the machinist trade, I guess. He also worked for some time as a meat cutter but later developed a problem with his heart, so he couldn't work around electrical equipment.

Ray was always the great white hunter of our family, though, and has probably hunted and fished every nook and cranny of the state of Oregon, although I don't know if he ever shot a nook or hooked any crannies. He actually found out about his heart problem when he blacked out and fell from a tree stand while bowhunting for deer. He retired on a disability pension in Albany, Oregon. After his son Joshua graduated and left home, Ray moved back to Lebanon, Oregon.

The Move to Oregon

In case you didn't catch this from the first chapter listing the Rogue's Gallery, I'll repeat myself. My mother was from a family of twelve kids, all of whom stayed in Texas as far as I know, except one. My uncle Roy joined the Navy during WWII and ended up in Oregon, where he married my aunt Agnes.

In 1951, my family and I, being the youngest at that time, still lived in Wheeler, Texas, which is just two or three sandstorms east of Amarillo. Since my dad was a lifelong farmer but had not seemed to raise much of anything except seven kids, my uncle Roy wrote (yes, actually had to put pen to paper back then) and said Dad could probably find a job in one of the sawmills in Oregon. He suggested that we make the move and even loaned Dad a little bit of money to make the trip.

So they loaded up the truck and moved to Beverly...oops, wrong bunch! But load up, we did. I said "we," but I was only four and one half, so I doubt if I did anything but get in the way. They took everything they could cram into a 1938 Chevy four-door sedan. We didn't have a rocking chair tied on top, but I'm sure Dad had something up there since he had himself, Mom, and the last five of us kids to put inside. Oh, and let's not forget the blue metal suitcase that was tied to the front of the car. With all that, the trunk full and a twelve-foot cane fishing pole tied along the side of the car, we set out for Oregon in June of that year. We may not have been the Beverly Hillbillies or characters from *The Grapes of Wrath*, but I'm sure we looked like them. Gladys was twenty-two years old by then and was married to Charlie, who was in the Air Force, somewhere in Florida. Bill, the oldest boy, had joined the Navy in 1949 and was either in Korea or just back from there.

Somewhere out in the middle of Nowhere, USA, Dad managed to run into a full-grown cow that didn't seem to understand that a 1938 Chevrolet actually had enough metal in it to hurt you! She didn't move out of the road, but Dad did slow down enough that he just bumped her, so no animals were injured in the making of this story. However, the metal suitcase on the front—well, that got scrunched pretty good. Mom saved that old suitcase, crumpled as it was, for all the years she lived in our house. I think she just liked the memories that went with it.

Now I don't know if one had anything to do with the other, but shortly after the close encounter of the bovine kind, the headlights went out on that old car (actually, it's a REALLY old car now, but come to think of it, it was only thirteen years old at the time). Anyway, since Dad had no knowledge of the electrical workings of a car and probably no tools aboard, the lights would have to wait until we got to Oregon. So as a consequence, we traveled by day and slept out on the ground during the dark hours, which are pretty short in June. I'm not sure, other than by the grace of God, why none of us ever ended up with a rattlesnake under our covers, but we didn't. One thing I remember though is that back then, the truckers were some of the nicest people on the highway. They would let us sleep all night peacefully, but when daylight came, they would politely toot their air horns as they passed, as if to say, "Get up! It's time to get going!"

Now you got to remember that any kind of treats for the kids on this trip was out of Dad's vocabulary. So I don't know if it was one of his temporary insanity moments, or if one of the older siblings had some money stashed, but someone along the way, during a gas stop, I presume, bought all the kids a candy bar. Keep remembering that I was only four (and a half) and hadn't seen too many candy bars up 'til then, so I guess I'll just blame it on the excitement of the moment. As I unwrapped my candy, for a reason only known to heaven, I held onto the wrapper and threw the candy bar out the window! Oh, the wailing and gnashing of teeth! According to everyone in the car, and they repeated it over and over every chance they got for years, I really put on a sobbing fit such that, just to shut me up, I guess, they all had to share some of theirs with me. But like I said, I suffered through the retelling of that incident at every family gathering, reminding me of what a dope I was. My older brothers used to say I was the smart one in the family. I had learned to walk when I was five—forward when I was ten!

After many days on the road, we did finally arrive in Oregon's Willamette Valley, and oh, did Mom think she had found the Garden of Eden! To go from the bleak desert of Texas to that lush green valley was beyond anything she had imagined.

The first place we lived was near a community called Shedd, where Dad and maybe the two oldest boys, Jim and Bob, worked in the hayfields for a farmer. My only recollection of that place was the night Bob's 4-H pig got out of his pen, and the whole darned family, except for Mom and me, was out running up and down the road in the dark.

Not too much later, we moved on up to the Crabtree area, which is somewhere between Lebanon and Albany. I think Jim had gone back east with a friend by then, but that's another story. That left Bob, who was fourteen at the time, to work with Dad in the mint fields. They hoed and harvested mint plants, which their employer hauled to his own processing mill. There, the mint was put into a huge vat and boiled to extract the juice, which he then sold as mint extract (go figure). Mom found out right away that the extract was much more potent than any of us knew. She baked a cake and put a few drops of it into the batter, but the mint flavor was so strong no one could eat it. That's when she learned that simply dipping a toothpick into the bottle then stirring that around in the batter was sufficient. I don't think in all her years that she ever used up that tiny bottle of mint extract.

It was somewhere during that time that Mom contracted a case of canning fever. As I said before, she thought she had landed in the original Garden, where blackberries grew all over the fence rows, apples and cherries grew all around, and there was any number of vegetables to be had. We used to say that we kids had to keep moving, or Mom would have put us in a quart jar. I still remember that she canned so many cherries during that time. We still had several jars left on the pantry shelf years later. I think she just canned so many of them. We refused to eat anymore!

Some of Dad's initial experiences in our new world were less than positive. First of all, everyone he met had to tell him that it was not the Will-a-**METTE** Valley, but it was the Will-**AM**-ette, and the state was not pronounced "OreeGON" but more like "Oragun." Then once, in asking directions to one of the farms, a man told him to go out to the middle of a certain bridge and TURN RIGHT! Well, Dad, of course, thought the guy was some sort of wisecracker, but as it turned out, the guy was serious. There was a long bridge over a very narrow creek, so about two-thirds of the way across, there actually was an off-ramp that went down to the guy's farm.

After working seasonal farmwork for about the first year, Dad finally did land a job, working at Santiam Lumber Company, a lumber mill in Sweet Home. Shortly after that, they bought the little house on McKinney Lane. I still remember Dad ranting and raving that he had to pay $50 a month for ten years for a house that only sold for $2,500 to start with! Little did anyone back then realize how humorous that would be later in life, but at the time, Dad was working for less than $2/hour. They lived in that same house until Mom sold it in the 1990s to move to assisted living.

Our House

I've tried in recent years to calculate just how big or small, as the case may be that house on McKinney Lane was. The best figure I can come up with is 20 feet wide and about 27 feet front to back, which I know is only 540 square feet, but I'm sure that's close. By today's standards, that's less than a lot of double garages!

By looking at old home movies and photos, I know that the kitchen was just wide enough between the cabinets and the living room wall to put chairs around a 4×6-foot dining table. And if anyone needed in or out from the back side, everyone had to stand up since there wasn't even enough room to slip behind the seated folks. At the other end of the kitchen, toward the bathroom door, sat the stove and water heater on the right side and the refrigerator on the left with just enough room to walk between them to the bathroom. Dad, sitting at his usual place at that end of the table, didn't even have to get up from his chair to reach the coffeepot on the stove, so we know it wasn't far! More about that coffee later.

When we first moved in, and for several years after, the kitchen stove was a woodburning stove. The firebox had metal pipes running through it and connections on the side that were plumbed to a small, perhaps 25 gallons, water heater! That was a rarity for that day, as very few woodstoves had the feature. It was my job to make sure every night, before dark preferably, that the woodbox in the living room was full and the one in the kitchen had plenty of "stove wood" in it. Now "stovewood" was different from the larger pieces of wood that went in the heating stove, in that it had to be small, about two inches square or smaller. That was because the firebox on the stove was small, maybe 8 or 9 inches square, and the pieces had to be shoved in from the top through one of the "eyes" or through the small front door. I never figured out if that was "stovewood," what was the other larger stuff? Just firewood, I guess. And then, of course, there had to be kindling, very small pieces of wood, to put in first to get the fire started. We got a double dump truckload of wood from the plywood mill every fall. The pieces were called peeler cores since they were what was left of a log after they peeled layers off to make the veneer for plywood. Back then, they would range in diameter from a foot to sometimes two feet. With more modern technology now, the log is peeled down to almost nothing. (I think they just slice up what's left for toothpicks.) Turning those chunks into useable sizes was another of our jobs.

Mom got up every weekday morning at about 4:00 a.m. to get the kitchen stove fire going, so when Dad got up at five, the water in the water heater was hot enough to wash up. She shocked Betty when they first moved in next door by telling her that she beat her husband up every morning. Betty hadn't learned our sick sense of humor yet.

Now the bathroom, that's a whole 'nother story. We called it the "walk-in, back out" bathroom, and it was said that it was so small you didn't have room to change your mind. Granted, I was a tall, lanky kid as a teenager, but I could literally sit on the throne, put my feet over in the bathtub, and reach the sink faucets to my right. And forget about a shower! Just that old bathtub—how I hated it. Since I left home for the military, I could probably count on my two hands the times I've been back in a tub, and maybe all ten of those were our visits back to the folks' house!

I don't know exactly how large the living room was, but I do know that Dad bought something the store called an area rug, and we called it wall-to-wall carpet! We had an old woodstove in the corner nearest the folks' bedroom, and oh, how good that old friend felt when we would come in from playing or from school half-frozen and sidle up next to it to get warm. I don't think there's the warmth of any kind that's as cozy as wood heat. Years later, in California, we had the pleasure of having a woodstove in our house, and it was the nicest feeling of warmth in the world. But I digress... The only other things there was room for in that living room were a TV in the other corner, a small, easy chair, and a sofa at the end of which sat a small table with an am radio on it.

About that TV—for about two years after we moved into the house, we didn't own a TV, so every Friday night, we would go to Uncle Roy's house in town so Dad could watch professional boxing, aka "the fights." Pro wrestling didn't come into its own until later, so that was the only big thing. I still remember that the fights were always sponsored by Gillette Blue Blades and Pabst Blue Ribbon beer. And once a week, Pauline and I would go up the street to a neighbor's house so we could watch the Green Hornet or one of those few action shows that was on back then. Then around 1954 or so, Dad's ego, or his conscience, got the best of him, and he sprang for a new Packard Bell black-and-white TV. Boy, we thought we were keeping up with the Rockefellers! But back to the house...

Our house had one, no, actually two interesting things that per- haps no other house around had—windows between the living room and my bedroom and between the folks' bedroom and Pauline's room! When the house was built, apparently, our bedrooms were the covered front porch. Then sometime before we bought it, the front was enclosed to make two rooms. However, the front door opened into my bedroom, so after a few years of that, Dad and Jim built a wall across my room to make an entry hallway. It was interesting, in that, on that particular day, Bob was asleep in my bed, and with all the sawing, hammering, etc., and the boards and tools all over the bed, he didn't seem to mind. Must have been out way too late last night! But those two windows never got removed. So if the curtain wasn't in the way, I could always take a peek into the living room from my bed, especially if the folks sat up to watch TV, and I had to go to bed. But in later years, it made things kind of interesting when we went back to visit and slept in Pauline's old room because Dad was in bed across the wall from us. Windows don't block much sound, and boy, could he snore!

That bedroom of mine was another piece of work. Ray and I shared a bed until I got to be a teenager and advanced to the room over the garage (another story). The bed was a double, and the whole room was about one foot longer than the bed. The door swung inward and cleared the bed by about six inches, so I'd say the room was about 7 feet long by about 7 feet wide. We had room for a small chest of drawers beside the door but no closet, so our clothes had to hang on hangers on wall hooks behind and on the door. Keep in mind that most kids back then didn't have a wardrobe that would make Elvis proud! About three outfits apiece usually did it, and since we didn't go to church, we didn't have dressy clothes, just school and play (the playclothes being last year's school clothes). And since Ray was six years younger than I, by the time he needed school clothes, I was almost old enough to move upstairs. Pauline's bedroom was slightly larger than mine since some of mine became the entry hall. Her door was just the right width to swing back and interlock with the knob on the front door, so it became the "night latch" for the front door later after she married and moved out. One interesting fact is that when I was little, I once asked Mom and Dad where the keys were to the front and back doors. They said they didn't know because no one locked their doors back then! Years later, when we came back to visit, I noticed that the back door had a new deadbolt installed, and the front door was always "locked" by using that bedroom door. How the times changed.

The exterior of our house was interesting, too, in that it never had a real foundation. The outside walls were log slabs, not whole logs, but just slabs from them, probably scavenged from one of the mills, as they cut all four sides off a round log to make a square "cant" or large piece of lumber to be cut up. The walls inside were plywood. I guess because Sheetrock hadn't come along yet. Anyway, as I said, the wooden walls sat in the dirt, so over the years, they started to rot, and we used to say the house would fall down if the termites ever quit holding hands! So every spring, after termite-mating season, we waited to see if it did, indeed, collapse. But I think by divine intervention, the darned thing kept standing until some years later when Dad and some of the brothers poured a cement curb along the side of the house and garage. Note that they didn't jack the house up and pour a foundation UNDER it, as that would have been a job for a contractor. I guess they thought if the walls had cement around them, they couldn't fall down...and they never did.

When we first moved into the house, it was kind of an unpainted wood brown, mainly because it was—unpainted! Shortly after we moved in, however, Dad must have gotten a real bargain on some dark-green, oil-based paint (water-based latex wasn't available yet). So for all the years following, that was the color it stayed, a dark forest green. And I will always remember that every time the outside or inside of the house was painted with that paint, it had a stink that seemed to last for a month. At one point in time, the bathroom was a flamingo pink, and the kitchen cabinets were chocolate brown. It was like living in a Baskin-Robbins!

The first few years we lived in the house, there was an old chicken house out in the back corner of the yard. We never had any chickens, so we used it as a woodshed. One night, a teenage boy who lived in the back of us cut through our yard to go into his back door since no one had any fences in those days. He didn't want his parents to know he was smoking, so as he walked through our yard, he tossed his lighted cigarette aside right next to that old shed! Being as dry as a powder horn, that building went up in flames in minutes. By the time the fire department got there, it was pretty much burned to the ground. We didn't find out what caused the fire until years later, when the neighbor boy confessed to Wayne. The good news was that Dad had homeowner's insurance, which paid him much more for that old run-down building than it was really worth, I'm sure.

The bad news was that Wayne had his 1947 Ford parked right up against the front of that old building! Not long before, he had pulled the engine out of it and was rebuilding it in his high school auto-shop class. It goes without saying that his car went up with the shed, becoming the first "Car-B-Que" I had ever seen. The rubber tires got so hot they burst into flame, which in turn burned the car to a crisp. I always wondered if Wayne got any of the insurance money from that or if Dad kept it all. All I know is that Wayne ended up later with another 1947 Ford sedan and a spare rebuilt engine.

Our garage consisted of a single-car space with dirt floor then a raised wooden floor area that attached the garage to the back corner of the house. That area later became a small tool shop for Dad and pantry shelves for Mom. At the same time, the dirt floor where the car sat was cemented. By the door going on out to the back porch sat the old wringer washing machine. Dad never would buy Mom an automatic washer because he thought they used too much water and didn't get the clothes clean anyway. That was the same Maytag machine that they had shipped to Oregon when we moved from Texas (the only thing that didn't come with us in the car). Initially, though, the machine had a very small gasoline engine with a kick pedal to start it, much like motorcycles had. To use it indoors, it had a metal flex hose that ran outside, so you didn't kill yourself off with carbon monoxide. Later, Mr. Got-Rocks splurged and had an electric motor put on it and even finally bought Mom an electric dryer. That was after he lived in Oregon long enough to find out they only had two seasons—the rainy season and the Fourth of July! Since he got tired of waiting for clean, dry overalls every year until the Fourth, he decided it was time for drastic measures…buy into the twentieth century!

That garage was too old to have a swing-up or roll-up door. Instead, there were two big wooden doors that swung back to each side. In good weather, they were always open. If anyone we knew, including any of the family, came to visit, they never came through the front door. They parked in, or next to, the driveway and entered through the garage and the back door, which was also open during the warm season. So if anyone knocked on our front door, we knew immediately it was a stranger and probably a salesman. Dad always said he was going to put a sign on the front door, saying, "We shoot every third salesman. The second one just left," but, of course, he never did. Once in a while, a railroad bum would knock on that front door, needing something to eat. Mom wouldn't allow them in the house, but she always had leftovers, which she put on a tin plate and gave them to eat on our front steps.

Before, I mentioned sleeping in the room over the garage. Just as you exited the garage to the back porch, there was a set of stairs to an upper room. Since we had five kids when we moved in (Ray wasn't born until 1953), there obviously wasn't room for all of them in the house, so the older boys slept upstairs. Then Jim left then Bob then Wayne, and I got old enough to move up there and had it all to myself for a while. But when Wayne got out of the Navy in 1961, he moved back home, so we shared the room until he went back into the Navy in 1964. Anyway, it had plenty of room for two double beds, so that was no problem. What WAS a problem was that it was the coldest place south of the North Pole in the wintertime. Insulation was pretty much nonexistent back then, not in the walls, and the ceiling was vaulted, which is a nice name for "there's no room for insulation there either." The floor was linoleum, so when it got really cold outside, it was pretty much the same inside. The wiring for that house was archaic, so all the room had was a bare-bulb droplight in the center of the ceiling with a pull-string. We tied the pull-string to the headboard of my bed so we could get in bed and cover up before we turned out the light. Prior to that, we were pulling the string and trying to get in bed before the light went out, but neither of us was fast enough! I remember doing my high school homework after I got home from Hackett's Texaco, where I worked most nights, sitting up in that bed, trying to stay warm. I doubled as Wayne's alarm clock since he worked the graveyard shift at the plywood mill but would stay up all day then get a few hours' sleep in the evening. It was my job to wake him up just in time for him to make a fifteen-minute dash to the mill every night at eleven.

McKinney Lane was a dead-end gravel road that traveled ever so slowly uphill to the far end and was about 300 yards long with a dozen or so houses on one side, facing a large vacant lot on the other side. Our misfortune was that we didn't live at the far end but were the second house in from Russell Drive, the paved road that was built up higher than our lane. So that left our end of the road in the lowest spot of all since all the property around us was higher ground also. In the winter, which was a name they gave to one quarter of the rainy season, the whole end of the road would usually flood and back up to our house. That meant that the "leach lines," the lines that were supposed to drain the water from the septic tank, would be full, and the water backed up, so the septic tank couldn't drain and would eventually fill up. We had a spring ritual that we called Septic Pumping, where the man would come out, pump the septic tank dry, and charge us more money.

But before we go on with the septic story, I have to digress. In the garage under the stairs sat an old piston-type well pump and pressure tank. The only reason the two of them hadn't come over on the Mayflower was that by then, better ones had been invented—at least that's my perception. Anyway, for the pressure tank to work properly, there had to be a cushion of air trapped up in the top of the tank, so when the water was pumped into it, that air could be compressed, hence the name "pressure tank." But over time, for some reason, the tank would lose its air, then the pump would run too much, and the pressure in the house would get even worse than usual. That was Dad's signal to get out the tire pump (the same one we used to pump up our bike tires), drain some water from the tank, and pump more air in. But even in the best of times, the pressure, by any standard, was poor. And that is where the septic tank story comes in.

One fine spring day, I guess it was during the celebration of Septic Pumping, sure enough, the guy was there, pumping the thing out. When he had pumped it most of the way, he had to add some water, presumably to dilute the "you-know-what" in the bottom. So he got the garden hose that lived by the back porch, stuck it in the hole, and asked Mom to turn on the water. Well, I guess he'd never seen water pressure that poor before, so he asked her to turn it all the way on. When she told him that was all it had, he said, "Lady, I can drink two beers and have more pressure than that!"

As you can imagine, Mom was pretty embarrassed by his remark and thought he was very rude. Secretly though, she must have thought it was funny because she never tired of telling the story.

That old well pump may not have been the greatest, but the water from the well was second to none. We had many visitors remark about how good our water tasted. And I would assume there is still plenty of it today since Dad was always trying to conserve, afraid our well would go dry. That was probably from his life in Texas, where the wells were all dug, not drilled, and since the climate was much drier, a lot of times, that did happen. As a result, all the years I lived at home, we were conscious of that need to save water. (I'm sure the conservationists of today would have been very proud of us.) Well (pardon the pun), years after I left home, that old pump started sucking air! Right away, Dad was sure he had been right all along, and the well was dry. But when he got an expert out to have a look, it turned out that the galvanized steel pipe coming up out of the well, being the original pipe and no telling how old, had developed a hole it from corrosion. The hole was above the water level down below, hence the air-sucking thing. While the guy was there, however, he also dropped some kind of device down the well and told the folks to stop worrying about ever being without water—they were sitting on an underground stream that was about 10 feet deep! A new piece of pipe slipped down inside the old one took care of the problem, but I don't think it changed Dad any. He had been the "Water Nazi" far too long to change. By then, though, I had my own house and didn't have to try to take a bath in two inches of water.

Oh, but remember that gas engine that used to run the washing machine? Ray informed me recently that after I left home, Dad put it to good use. He rigged a pulley on it that would run the well pump during power outages—Yankee ingenuity?

Mom's Cooking

All the time we were growing up, we always thought we were deprived because Dad didn't make very much money, so we subsisted mainly on beans and potatoes and sometimes meat on Sunday. Years later, we were to realize that we were probably much healthier from that diet than the people who had richer foods and lots of red meat to eat. An Asian friend of mine once told me his mom always had a pot of cooked rice on her stove to serve no matter what else they were having for the meal. Well, that's how my mom was with pinto beans. We called them red beans, although they are technically more brown than red. If you were to enter our house any day of the week, she had a big pot of beans cooking on the stove. And more likely than not, a pan of fried potatoes would be cooked that evening to go with them. With most dinners ("supper" to those of you from the South), Mom would make corn bread, and we would have a variety of fresh vegetables if they were in season or something canned if they were not. We ate a lot of green beans in August since Wayne, Pauline, and I all worked in the bean field, so we would always bring home a couple of handfuls to cook for dinner. But there were also many gardens in our neighborhood, one very large one being the vacant lot next door. The owner, Mr. Rush, was always generous with his tomatoes, carrots, radishes, and anything else he grew.

We were very fortunate in the fact that we rarely ate store-bought bread. Besides the corn bread for dinner, Mom always made biscuits for breakfast. Since all of us, except Mom, were away at lunch during the week, we took sandwiches made of "light bread," the folks' name for sliced store bread. I have to assume that was because it was inherently "lighter" than homemade bread since they didn't know why they called it that either! Anyway, with the breakfast biscuits, we usually had bacon and eggs. Yes, over the years, we probably ate enough eggs to wipe out a large Foster Farms plant, and any hog worth his bacon wouldn't come within a mile of our house. If there was time, there was also white gravy for the biscuits. Now as if these were not enough to start your arteries hardening until I was in my teen years, Mom also cooked everything in real lard! I know a lot of people think of lard as ugly and repulsive, but actually, it's a beautiful white color, and you couldn't tell it from the solid form of Crisco until you tasted the results. Everything tasted better cooked in lard! I know that's probably what shortened both Mom and Dad's lives—after all, Dad only lived to be eighty-nine, and Mom passed too soon at ninety-eight!

Mom's biscuit method was something of a legend among the ladies in the family, at least to several of the daughters-in-law. You see, our old kitchen had two swing-out bins at the end of the cabinets by the back door. These bins were quite large and metal-lined, so that's where Mom stored her baking goods. In those days, sugar was only bought by the ten-pound bag since we didn't really eat a lot of sweets. Cornmeal was bought 25 pounds at a time and flour by the 50-pound bag. (Potatoes, by the way, were bought in 100-pound bags.) The sugar, cornmeal, and flour went into the metal bins to keep mice and bugs from getting into them. And on the right side, where the flour was, there was always a big plastic bowl. To make her biscuits, Mom scooped that bowl about half full, made a large crater in the middle of it, and all the fixins—baking powder, water, salt, etc.—went right into that depression. Then with her hand, she slowly worked the flour into the wet ingredients until it was a nice ball of dough. She never rolled that out and cut the biscuits. She just pinched off pieces and formed them into the right shape! I remember my wife Sharon watching this procedure several times and marveling at the method and the fact that Mom didn't measure anything. The recipe was burned into her mind from the hundreds of times doing that same thing. The amazing thing was every batch came out the same—time after time.

Mom was very good at making the things she had made over and over, but there were things like cakes that she never got very good at. That was mainly because she didn't do it very often and also because Dad wouldn't buy the boxed mixes. That meant she had to make them from scratch, as they say, and I remember some baked goods we could easily have used for a boat anchor. We always ate whatever she made and didn't complain, however. Maybe it was because of the plaque that hung on the kitchen wall, right over the dining table, that read, "Warning: complaints to the cook can be hazardous to your health." That was more of Mom's silly sense of humor. At least, that's what I always told myself.

However, we could always depend on the basics, and it was comforting to know that when we got up for school, there was always a hot breakfast waiting. Or when we came home from school, starving as most kids are, there was that aroma of hot food cooking on the stove. My brothers and I have often laughed about the fact that we couldn't wait to leave home and get something different to eat. But after a few months away, when we entered the military, we would have given a month's pay just to taste Mom's beans and corn bread or biscuits and gravy again!

I mentioned before that most of our diet was beans and potatoes, but if we were fortunate enough to bring home a deer or two during hunting season, the venison supplemented our meals too. Mom sure could make great steak and gravy out of that! In most years, there was at least one deer in the freezer, sometimes two, and we ate that as long as it lasted. Or, if the budget permitted, Dad would buy chicken, pork chops, or a beef roast, which was saved for Sunday dinner.

The reason I said Dad bought it is because Mom never went to the store! She never learned to drive, and Dad never took her with him to buy groceries. As strange as it seems, I guess they formed that habit back when they lived out in the country, and she couldn't leave a small herd of kids alone to go on a long ride to town. Anyway, she would make up the grocery list, and Dad would go to the store every Saturday morning. For years, he drove back out to Crabtree, which was about a fifteen-mile drive to Knight's General Store, even though there was any number of food stores right there in town. It seems that when we first moved to Oregon, Mr. Knight gave Dad credit to buy groceries before he had a steady job at the mill. So out of loyalty to a good friend, he continued to buy at Mr. Knight's store until years later when Knight had to retire, and the store closed.

Once in a while, I got to go with Dad to buy the groceries, and it was such an adventure! Mr. Knight's store was truly a general store since he had groceries, a fresh meat counter, sporting goods, even guns for sale, and gas pumps out front. But the thing that intrigued me was a big back room where there were tables and tables of every kind of gadget and contraption you could think of. Today, it would be called a collectibles fair, I guess, but then it was just a lot of interesting junk. I would spend every minute I could while Dad was buying the groceries, exploring, always finding something that piqued my curiosity.

The one thing that would get me out of that back room in a hurry though was if Dad volunteered to buy us both a cold Coke from Mr. Knight's cooler. This was no coin-operated vending machine full of cans. This was a chest-type soft drink cooler that circulated ice-cold water over and around real glass bottles! Now keep in mind that this didn't happen on every trip, but once in a while, I think Dad had a craving for a nice cold drink, even though he would never have admitted it. Whatever the reason, it was a treat that I never forgot, that 12 ounces of ice-cold Coke, so cold it had little flakes of ice in it as it passed over my tongue. I sure did miss those trips to Knight's General Store when it closed!

Meanwhile, back to Mom's cooking:

There was one other item besides that perpetual pot of beans that would always be found on Mom's kitchen stove. That would be a large percolator coffee pot, a twenty-cupper, perched on the back burner and always hot and ready to drink. As soon as the woodstove was hot in the morning, that pot went on to perk, and it was there all day. Visitors, usually my brothers, always came in the back door, and the first thing they did was go for a cup of coffee.

Dad and Mom were both big coffee drinkers, and until much later in life, it wasn't your namby-pamby, weak-sister stuff. No, this was what Dad always liked to call Texas Coffee, and according to him, if a spoon didn't stand alone in a cup of it, you probably needed to perk it longer—just a slight exaggeration perhaps, but not by much. That coffee would put hair on a rock, or if the rock had hair, it would probably burn it off. It's funny, too, because years later, they were both drinking a much weaker brew of decaf. Was it because the real thing started to affect their sleep, or did they finally realize that their stomach lining was half gone?

For some reason, Dad always thought we kids should not drink coffee (truth be known, it was probably because it left less for him). Anyway, I don't know if I actually liked the taste of coffee or if it was all the cream and sugar I added to it. But so as not to bring on the "Twenty Reasons Why Kids Shouldn't Drink Coffee," I would make up my concoction over by the stove, where he couldn't see me from his usual spot on the couch. Then I would stand over by the bathroom door to drink it. Mom, of course, knew what I was doing, but she wasn't about to poke a stick at a hornet's nest, so she just kept it to herself. She did tell me several times that the stuff would stunt my growth—until I passed six feet tall, that is. I think I was at least a teenager before I could openly drink coffee. The irony of that, I guess, is that by that time, I was smoking too. But Dad didn't know about that until several years later. Parents in those days didn't hover over their kids. The kids were to take responsibility for themselves and suffer the consequences if they did wrong—if and when they got caught, of course! I guess that's why Dad used to say if we hadn't done whatever he was spanking us for, then it was for all the times he didn't catch us! I never saw the humor in that.

Mom's Medicines

If you thought Mom's menu was somewhat eccentric, let's discuss her medicinal remedies. Now I know, looking at some of these from today's perspective, you're going to think Mom was Dr. Kavorkian's assistant, but I swear, none of us ever suffered any adverse effects. None, that is, that can be differentiated from the lunacy we were all afflicted with anyway.

One of her favorite tricks was for a cold, sore throat, or anything that resembled any of them. That was to put a small lump of Vicks salve (aka Vicks VapoRub) on your tongue at bedtime and make you hold it there until it dissolved. Then while that was happening, she would take another lump of it and rub it all over your chest. Now the part she put on our chest burned a little bit, but we could live with that. It was that part that melted and went down our throat that was bad. The amazing thing about it, though, was that it seemed to work. We would always wake up the next morning feeling better.

A very old remedy for injuries was kerosene! I wasn't born at the time, but I heard the account of the time Bill stepped on a nail in a board, so that it went most of the way through his foot. After pulling the nail out, Dad held him down while Mom poured the puncture full of kerosene, then they wrapped the foot in a clean cloth soaked in kerosene. Even though it sounds horrendous, the foot healed up just fine, and Bill was no worse off for that strange remedy. There were many other cuts, scrapes, and gouges that Mom applied kerosene to until later in our lives when another product came out called Oil of Salts. This was a commercial product, but I'm still not sure that the key ingredient wasn't kerosene—it smelled just like it! Whatever. Mom used that on my little finger the time I was chasing Ray alongside the house and ran my little finger along the barbed wire fence that separated our yard from Mr. Rush's vacant lot. That cut went almost to the bone and was the length of my finger. Out came the Oil of Salts, which she applied liberally to the wound then wrapped the finger tightly with a clean piece of cloth. At the time, I was still going to the doctor's office one Saturday a month for my bicillin shot. That Saturday happened to be just a few days later, so Dr. Reid took a look at my finger. All he said was that the cut should have been sewn up, but by then, it was too late. Other than that, he said it was healing nicely. Today, I don't even have enough scar to brag about.

I don't remember us ever having iodine in the house, but we had something like it, except that it burned much worse. It was the devil's concoction called Merthiolate, and I'm not sure which was worse—the injury or the cure. I don't think they even make that reddish, watery stuff now since most of the products on the market like to brag that they are ouchless or painless. After all, we can't have our kids subjected to any discomfort now. It would probably bring on post-traumatic stress disorder in most of them. Well, anyway, if Merthiolate ever had a TV commercial, which I doubt, that would not be included in their claim to fame. I suppose they could have called it iodine with an attitude! But like all the other items in Mom's medicine chest, it seemed to do the trick.

Oh yes, and never, I mean, never tell Mom you had a stomach-ache, constipation, or anything that even sounded like an intestinal disorder! She had this bottle of thick, dark-colored liquid that I'm fairly sure had a skull and crossbones on it. That wonderfully delicious remedy was called castor oil, and she would give you a teaspoon of it if you even looked cross-eyed! To this day, I wonder if it was given as a medicinal aid or as a punishment for all the things she knew we did but didn't get caught at. It wasn't that it did your body any good so much as it was so gosh-awful-tasting. Your body would hurry up and heal itself to avoid a second dose. I have no firsthand knowledge of castor oil ever curing anyone. But I know I never went back for seconds. It was a case of mind over matter, I think.

Our Neighborhood

I mentioned that McKinney Lane was a gravel road. Just to show how different things were back then, every summer, usually, several times during the dusty season (yes, we had dust when it didn't rain), Mr. Weller, who lived up at the other end of the street and who had elected himself the mayor of McKinney Lane, had some kind of waste liquid from the paper mill brought out and sprayed on our road to keep the dust down. I never quite knew what the composition of that liquid was, but I have a feeling if two tablespoons of it were spilled on the road today, there would be a federal hazmat team of forty guys there to make sure it didn't contaminate the environment! It did a great job of keeping the dust out of our houses, though, and as far as I know, or that anyone could prove in court, no one ever died from it. However, for several days after the spraying, you could taste this foul, metallic taste in your mouth. I'm sure it was perfectly harmless though.

All the houses along McKinney Lane faced that big open vacant lot, which in spring would grow up about waist-high to a basketball center with grass. Many a day has been spent by my friends and me, carefully crawling in and around, back and forth in a zigzag pattern, making a trail out to the middle of that field to make ourselves a fort or playhouse or whatever that little matted-down area needed to be on that occasion. We made several large rooms, joined by narrow passageways, and spent countless hours just enjoying our hideout. Of course, I have to come clean and admit that when we got to somewhere around eleven or twelve years old, part of the rite of passage to our teens was to use that hideout to experiment with smoking! It's not something that I'm proud of, but that was the '50s! Just about everyone we knew smoked, and cigarettes were promoted in the media as if they were the best thing that ever happened to mankind. Jack Webb of the TV and radio show *Dragnet* was heard pushing cartons of Chesterfields at Christmas time as gifts for all your friends. Anyway, what we put in our mouths and lit wasn't always a store-bought cigarette or "ready-roll." It ran the gamut from a parent's pipe tobacco rolled crudely in a paper made for home-rolled cigarettes to the seeds from a plant we called "Indian tobacco," crushed and rolled up in paper. I guess the only reason we didn't kill ourselves off is that, as novice smokers, we couldn't inhale. Oh, you might try it once, but it had the equivalent feeling of shoving a dry corncob down your throat then pouring alcohol on it. Sometimes, it amazes me that anyone ever conquers the habit of smoking since it is so painful at first! But at least, to our credit, I can say we never caught the field on fire, which is a small miracle in itself.

Beyond that vacant, grass-covered lot were the railroad tracks that ran through our town but also had spurs or sidings for loading lumber and plywood from all the mills. Back in those days, you could hardly throw a rock around town without hitting at least one mill. About a half mile to our southeast was Cascade Plywood, then just about two hundred yards to our north was McPherson's Lumber Mill. As a matter of fact, the millpond where they dumped the logs while they awaited their fate in the mill started right at the end of McKinney Lane, just across Russell Drive. From our mailboxes, where we waited for the school bus through eighth grade, you could easily lob a rock over into the pond, which we did as a pastime every school morning. I think the adults often wondered why there was never any gravel in front of the mailboxes. Or you could watch as loads of logs came in on the trucks, where they were hooked to a big cable and pulled off the truck and into the pond. Wow! What a splash they made, as six or eight huge tree trunks hit the water! At night, I could sit on the front step and see the glow of the burner, its conical shape looking like a giant red-blazing tepee, lighting up the sky and sending glowing embers floating upward. All the scrap wood and sawdust were consumed there before anyone thought of making them into particleboard.

There were several more lumber mills around the area, as well as Crown-Zellerbach paper mill on the north edge of town. Just about everyone I knew worked in one of the mills or was a logger that helped supply the mills. That was what made up our town back then. I can still see several men from our street early in the morning, walking down to catch their bus or "crummy" that took them up to the logwoods, as their jobsite was called. They all had on those really tough denim pants held up with suspenders, their leg cuffs looking too short and all jagged at the bottom. It wasn't a fashion statement. They cut the bottom hems off and shortened them well above their boots to prevent getting their pant leg caught on a tree limb which could result in injury or death. The boots were actually called "calked boots" because of the steel studs all over the soles and heels, made so their foot didn't slip off when walking on a log. But we mistakenly called them "cork boots." It was years later before I knew what the heck corks had to do with their boots. Okay, to be honest, I must confess that I hardly, if ever, saw them walking TO their crummies since they had to leave at about three in the morning to get to the jobsite by daylight. I may have heard them some summer mornings since, in warm weather, I had my bedroom window open. But I did see them coming back down the street in the evening, looking very tired and dirty, their heavy boots going crunch, crunch, crunch in the gravel. There would be an old metal lunch box under their arm and, if they were lucky, a thermos bottle, dented and missing most of its paint, in their hand.

Along the railroad track beside McPherson's mill, there was a loading dock, a long raised platform where the lumber carriers, called "jitneys," could bring stacks of lumber to be loaded into the side door of a train car. The end nearest the street was a ramp for the jitneys to drive up, but the other end was, well, just the end—no rail, no fence, just a six-foot drop to the ground! One of our favorite sports was to see who could race their bike from the ramp end to the other end, slam on their brake, and stop the closest to the edge. Lonnie, a kid some two years older than I, to put it nicely, was a stout boy. As a result, he rode a big, stout bicycle, and he loved this sport. One day, although I was not that daring, I got lucky and stopped about a foot from the edge. Well, Lonnie couldn't be outdone since he WAS daring (he ended up in prison much later for stealing someone's pickup!), so he raced even faster than usual and slammed on the coaster brake of that big burly bike. But with all that momentum, all that bulk was not going to stop on a dime, and off he went, sailing through the air with the greatest of ease. Yes, the sailing was easy, but, as they say, that sudden stop at the bottom didn't exactly make his day. He did manage to stay upright and landed that Huffy bicycle on its wheels. But even with the oversized cushy seat he had installed for his big tushy, the impact must have rattled his teeth! He forced a smile and said in a high, soprano voice, "I'm okay," but he never asked me to play chicken on the loading dock ever again. And that suited me just fine since the sight of his flight gave me nightmares for a while.

The Welfare House

I said our house was the second one on our street. The first one, when we moved there, was occupied by the Arts family. Bob, the dad, was one of those loggers I mentioned, and they were a nice family with a girl and boy about Pauline's and my age, respectively. The mom's misfortune was that her first name was Fern, which was just fine, except when the junk mail came. I know we've all seen the junk mail, called "circulars" or "boxholders," addressed to J. Jones or S. Smith. Well, to her chagrin, her junk mail came addressed to F. Arts, which to our dirty little minds was hilarious. Nowadays, with the X-rated movies sold as PG-13 and four-letter words taken for granted, it would be no big deal, but to our naive, sheltered minds, it was a riot, from which we managed to get a lot of chuckles!

One day, Pauline and Jeanette, Johnny Arts's older sister, were playing dolls in a little house in their backyard. Near the door of that house were a truck tire and wheel, fully inflated, making it a perfect target for Johnny and me to throw rocks at. The trick was to see who could bounce a rock the farthest by hitting the tire. Well, as luck would have it, a fire truck went by just as I bounced a rock very nicely off that tire. Pauline stuck her head out the door to see where the truck was going, just in time for that rock to bounce up and hit her in the forehead. So if you ever saw her later, she had a nice scar above one eye, about half-inch long. Of course, Mom didn't seem to see my point—that it was just a random event in the universe—and tanned my little hide for throwing rocks at my sister! However, just a few years before, when we lived in a rented house over on Center Street, she hit me in the forehead with a tin can while we were playing a game called, ironically, Kick the Can. I have an identical scar above my eye! But for some reason, Mom just called that an accident, and no one got punished. Go figure.

Bob Arts drove a 1949 blue Oldsmobile Rocket 88, which was, for its time, very fast. Like many loggers, Bob was a daredevil, which was pretty much a prerequisite for his vocation. One of the things he liked to do with that Olds 88 was to floorboard it when he hit the blacktop on Russell Drive and see how fast he could go before he got to US Highway 20, the main route into town. The distance was probably more than that, but to Bob, it was his quarter-mile drag strip! That would have been fine, considering the traffic at that time wasn't much, but he did it several times with his son and me in the car. We, of course, thought it was the greatest of fun, too young to even realize the possible outcome if he failed to stop. But he always did. It was much later in my young life before I told my mom about it. I knew if she knew, she'd probably bend a frying pan over Bob's head.

After a few years, the Arts family moved on, and we never had another stable resident there as long as I lived at home. The house became the welfare house, one family after another of ne'er-do-wells, living off the taxes of those who did work, working the system instead of a job.

One guy who stands out in my memory was collecting welfare because he said he had a bad back. Yet while he was on welfare, he spent his days climbing trees in the woods with climbing boots, stripping slabs of green moss off the trees, all of which could weigh fifty to one hundred pounds apiece. He then took the moss home, put it in a big wire tumbler, tumble dried it, and sold the result to the local plant nurseries. We always wondered, if his back could stand that kind of abuse, why he wasn't able to work at a regular job?

Another family who lived in the house for a few years was a single mom, although I have to use the term "mom" loosely, with six kids, stairstepped in age, the oldest being probably twelve. They lived in the house with very little of the amenities we all take for granted. The first of every month, when the welfare check came, the mom dressed up in a sleek black dress, I guess the only one she owned. She told the kids she was "going to church" but didn't come back until some time the next day. One of those times, when their mom was gone, one of the little boys cut his foot. Having nowhere else to turn, one of his brothers came to our house for help. I was probably twelve or more, so Mom sent me over to take care of it. You could not imagine the filth, the squalor, that those children lived in! There was very little furniture, mattresses were on the floor, or just bedding on the floor itself, and I think a raggedy old couch on one wall. I did patch up the injured foot, but my curiosity got the best of me, wondering just what that mother had left those kids to live on. I looked into a small refrigerator and was shocked to see absolutely nothing, except a half-full jar of peanut butter! Sometime later, she must have spent too much money at "church" because the landlord forced her to move out, which was a relief to all of us.

The last ones I remember to live in that house were the Pattersons. I don't recall much at all about the parents, but they had two boys. The older one, Dick, was just a little older than I but had already spent one term in the boys' detention home or as it was locally known just "Woodburn." Woodburn was actually a real city north of us on I-5, but for some reason, if anyone was talking about a boy being sent away, it was said he was "sent up to Woodburn," and it went without interpretation that he went to be incarcerated. I don't think Dick had a very happy homelife because he told me once that the only place he really felt comfortable was when he was locked up. Perhaps he was abused at home. At my age, that never occurred to me. But one Saturday, much to my surprise, my dad asked me if I would like Dick to go fishing with us. Well, since Dad was not exactly known to us as a social worker of the year, I was shocked. But I did ask, and Dick went with us fishing. I was young then and didn't really think too much about it at the time, but later in life, I got to thinking that was probably the highlight of Dick's young life—just to be with someone who cared enough to treat him to a fishing trip. As I said, Dad's usual philosophy was "live and let live" and mind your own business, so the invitation didn't happen again. I often wondered how much different Dick would have turned out if we could have continued an interest in him. Dick eventually went back to Woodburn then was transferred to adult prison. He got out some years later, and I heard he was murdered.

The Koenig/Hackett House

Next door to us on the other side was a house that was built long before we moved there by a German man named Ted Koenig (he told me it was German for "king," and he pronounced it that way). I don't know if there was a hill in that spot already or if he had about a gazillion yards of dirt delivered. However it came about, his house and the one on the other side of him, which he also built, sat on ground that was 5 or 6 feet higher than anyone else's yard. The basement of the house started at about the same level as our yard, so just the top 2 feet or so stuck up above ground level, allowing for windows into the basement. On the front of the house, on our side, the garage was also underground and had a large room at the back of it. Mr. Koenig had designed the house with a furnace in the basement, and it was fueled with sawdust! Back then, with all the mills in the area, a truckload of sawdust could be bought for very little money since it was a by-product that they would have burned at the mill anyway. I used to watch as the big truck would pull up next to one of the windows into that back room, stick a large flexible tube through the window, and blow all that sawdust in! There was no fancy delivery system to his furnace. Ted simply went down to the basement when necessary, took a large shovel, and put the sawdust into the furnace firebox. I always wondered how he managed to burn sawdust that was from green wood and usually wet. Maybe he had a source to get seasoned-dry sawdust.

The house had no central fan and no air ducts. The ceiling of the basement had louvered registers into the rooms above it, and the ceiling of the first floor had more of these into the rooms of the upstairs. These louvers could be opened or closed to regulate how much heat was delivered from the basement, strictly by convection.

A few years after we moved in, Ted Koenig sold his house to the Hackett family. They were a nice young family, and although the parents were a whole generation younger than mine, they had two young daughters. Nancy was my age, and Becky was Ray's age. When they first moved in, Dave, the dad, worked at the plywood mill but later bought the Texaco station out on the I-5 freeway and ran that until long after I left home. I worked my way through high school working for him at the station.

I mentioned that the garage of that house was subterranean. It was all made of concrete, including the roof, which was flat, so it served as a perfect patio right outside their front door at the same level. The roof patio had a kind of lattice rail around it, so that meant they could sit out there in the summer months and entertain themselves listening to the Leards next door. Since no one had air conditioning in that part of the country back then, plus the fact that everyone smoked, the "menfolk" of our family always sat outside at an old picnic table my folks had. The houses faced east, so the afternoons were usually spent in the driveway where it was shady, just in front of the garage doors. Back then, those doors stayed propped open day and night during the summer months. Our being situated there meant we were less than a stone's throw from the ears up on the roof patio. Betty, the mom, mentioned many times things that they overheard. Like the fact that all the Leard brothers delighted in cutting down each other, in fun, of course. It was usually a contest to see who could come up with the best and funniest insult. For instance, I was the only son over six feet tall with size 12 feet. I got things like, "You'd have been seven feet tall if you hadn't folded so much under at the bottom," or, "You have a great understanding. Too bad it's too far from your head." Last but not least, "Why don't you save money on shoes and just wear the boxes mine came in?"

Well, I guess Dave didn't have the same relationship with his brothers. Betty remarked to Mom once that he said if he and his brothers talked to each other the way we did, they would have either killed each other or not spoken to each other again! To us, it was all in good fun, and, of course, we knew if they were on that patio, they could hear everything we said—but we didn't care.

Our Town

Lebanon, Oregon, in the '50s was a town of just over five thousand people. Wayne used to say he remembered exactly what the population was when we moved there—5,280, the same as the number of feet in a mile. As I said, the town subsisted mainly on the lumber industry, so one can surmise that we didn't have a lot of sophistication there. But it was a nice town, and we even had a sign at the city limits, saying Lebanon was "The town that friendliness built." We lived out in the suburbs to the south of town, but it was less than a mile to the city center. That meant it wasn't difficult to walk into town to shop, go to the movies, bowling alley, or skating rink. We had two main streets through the heart of town, the four-lane street at the south end splitting at what we all called "the Y" into two lanes going north called Park Street, and two lanes coming south made Main Street. Back then, we had two movie theatres, Park Theater halfway down Park Street and the Kuhn Theater, right on downtown Main Street. Admission was 35¢, popcorn and drinks were 10¢! I was told that the Park Theater closed after I left town.

Back down on the four-lane section, there was the skating rink (I was only there a couple of times; I found the floor to be too hard), an A & W Drive-In, used car lots, gas stations, a little mom-and-pop grocery called Nameless Market, and Tasty-Freeze. Sometime during my grade school days, they changed the name to Hasty-Freeze, but it was still just a little drive-up place that had about the best frosties in town, which was what we called soft-serve cones. There were, of course, other businesses, but they were ones that didn't interest us. Across from the Hasty-Freeze was a little hamburger place called Ritchie's Drive-In.

Not only was Ritchie's "the place" to go for a hamburger or chili fries or whatever tickled your fancy, but it served as the turnaround spot for all the cars that were "dragging the gut" on Friday and Saturday nights. Dragging the gut later lost its glamour when it simply became "cruising," but back then, if you had a car, you would be found turning around at Ritchie's, going back up Park Street, turning back to Main at the north end of town, going north to the Dairy Queen, turning around, and driving back down Main to Ritchie's again. Then, of course, with occasional stops to get a Coke or food and see who was there with their cool car, you repeated the loop from dusk until either you ran low on gas or until Ritchie's closed. It wasn't the loop that was the fun—it was to see and be seen by every teenager with wheels!

The old guy Bill, a retired Navy chief petty officer, owned and ran Ritchie's, and he tolerated everyone turning around in front of his place because he knew that for every so many time around town, we were going to pull in and have something to eat or drink. You could park and go inside, which consisted of a small area in the middle to cook and serve the counter and a row of barstools in a "C" shape around the center area to sit on. There was the requisite jukebox over in one corner, of course, and you could play records, singles called "45s," for 10 cents a pop or three for a quarter. If you weren't that social, you could park, turn on your headlights, and the carhop would come out and take your order. The food tray hooked on your driver's window, and you turned on your lights again when you wanted it picked up. Ritchie's was where the coolest cars could be found, and many an evening was spent around them, talking engines, carburetion, exhaust systems, chrome wheels, or the best tuck-and-roll upholstery.

Just because you stayed in your car to eat didn't mean you missed out on the jukebox music. Ritchie's had an awning around the three sides in front where the cars parked, so you and your food were covered if it rained or in the shade if it was hot (topless restaurants were never very popular in Oregon). All around the outside, there were hi-fi speakers, playing whatever was on the jukebox. Even if you didn't stop, as you pulled in to turn around, you would hear the sounds of Elvis, Everly Brothers, Jerry Lee Lewis, Buddy Holly, Beach Boys, The Ventures, The Four Seasons, or any number of others, drifting out across the air, welcoming you in.

There were no weirdo bands screaming out junk no one could understand with inane names like Smashing Pumpkins or Grateful Dead. It was before all the "critters" made their way over from the UK, e.g., Beatles, Animals, Byrds, Yardbirds, etc. Nor were any of them chanting rhyming lines about killing cops or beating up your girlfriend. No, these were real songs with real music and words everyone could understand, likely as not love songs. Oh, there were a few where the car got stuck on the railroad track, and the Teen Angel died, trying to retrieve her boyfriend's class ring, or a car crash where the girl was dying, and her date could only get one Last Kiss. And the Everly Brothers waited for Ebony Eyes to arrive, only to have her die in a plane crash. That was about as bad as it got. The other 99 percent were pleasant, even happy songs that made you feel good, songs you could sing along with.

One night, as three of us were going back through town, I was driving. We had just stopped at Ritchie's for a large Coke, which had no snap-on lid and straw like they have now. I managed to make it all the way up Park Street and turn left at the end, back to Main. As I turned right again to go toward Dairy Queen, I was both steering and holding my Coke, still full, with my left hand. For some reason, I looked away a bit too long until one of the guys gave out a loud gasp. I looked up just in time to find myself over the centerline, facing a very large log truck coming right at us. Instinctively, without thinking about the drink, I swerved back into my own lane and avoided the collision but dumped that whole Coke in my lap, crushed ice and all! Needless to say, it was pretty embarrassing, parked at the curb, standing on the traffic side of my car, trying to get that sticky Coke and ice out of my crotch. And all the while, teens were driving by, hooting and shouting all sorts of remarks at me. I sure did dread going back to school the next Monday!

Another place I always loved was downtown. It was Durlam's Bakery, and anytime you got anywhere near downtown Main Street, that aroma from the bakery would pull you in, wafting through the air with the attraction of a siren's song, telling you that you just had to come in for a glazed doughnut or better yet, a maple bar! They had a small counter where you could sit and enjoy your choice of pastry with coffee. Doughnuts were a nickel. maple bars may have been as high as a dime, and a dime also bought you all the coffee you could drink. It was one of our regular stops anytime we were in the downtown area.

Down on the corner from the bakery was Johannsen's Drugstore, and in those days, I don't think the pharmacy sold half as much as the soda fountain they had inside. Again, it was just one small row of barstools with a serving area behind it, but you could get just about any flavor of Coke you could imagine—cherry, lemon, chocolate, and on and on. If you have never had a chocolate Coke, don't knock it until you've tried it. And, of course, you could get any number of flavors of milkshakes, ice cream floats, banana splits, or anything else that was made with ice cream. You never called a soft drink a "soda" since back then, that was a treat made up of ice cream and carbonated water. It was either a "soda pop" or simply "a Coke." There were no-diet drinks, no caffeine-free drinks, just the old standbys—Coke, Pepsi, Royal Crown Cola, root beer, and several flavors of fruity drinks, like Nehi Grape or Orange Crush.

At the south of town, we had a drive-in movie theatre called the Motor-Vu. I didn't get to go there very many times until I got old enough to take my own car or go with someone who had one. But a few times, in his weaker moments, Dad did take us to see a double feature. The one I remember most was Elvis Presley's very first movie, *Love Me Tender*. Looking back, I guess I'd have to say it was kind of a corny movie, but at that time, Elvis was the hottest and the coolest entertainer in the world, so to get to see him in a movie was an extra special treat. Add to that the fact that Dad actually took us to see it made it even better.

Before I got my first car, there was a guy named Rick that lived a few blocks from me. He was three or four years older than my two buddies and I, so he had an old 1949 Chevy coupe. We used to all pile into that old rattletrap when it decided to run, that is, and go to the Motor-Vu on what they called "Dollar a Carload" night. It's hard today to realize that we got four people in to see two movies and a whole bunch of cartoons for one dollar! That was the trade-off for all the times we had to push that old Chevy to get it going. But we always made those times fun, laughing and making jokes about Rick's car, like telling him it was so ugly he had to sneak up on a pump just to get gas. But secretly, we were just jealous because he had a car, and we didn't.

School

In the beginning, I mentioned that I went grades one through six to Crowfoot Elementary, which was named for the way the road branched three ways in front of the school. For grades seven and eight, I went to Seven Oaks Junior High and nine through twelve at Lebanon Union High School. So I'm not going to tell you all that again. Too late? Oh well, if you're like me, you needed to be reminded anyway.

I guess everyone in the lower grades always feels that their teachers are old—the term being relative to their age. What I learned years later was a real shocker, and it was that most of my grade schoolteachers were in their twenties and thirties when I was there!

It seems peculiar now with so much schoolwork being done on computer screens and handheld devices, but we actually learned our lessons on paper and on the blackboard. One of the little chores we shared at the end of each day was to take all the blackboard erasers down to the boiler room and clean them on a vacuum cleaner. The boiler room doubled as the teacher's lounge (can you see the teacher's union going for that now?). I can still see them sitting around the table when I came in...smoking! It shouldn't have shocked me since just about everyone smoked back then, but for some reason, I held teachers on a higher pedestal than that. In those days, they were never allowed to let the students see them smoking, so I guess I thought they didn't. I think they were a bit embarrassed, too, to have me see them. Perception has certainly changed with time.

There was only one time I can recall getting punished in school—I was pretty timid as a child, so I stayed out of trouble. But that one day, it was lunchtime, and I got up to throw away my garbage after eating. When I came back to my desk, the kid next to me thought it would be funny to move my chair, so he did. I missed the mark and sat with a big thud on the floor, which brought a round of laughter from the whole room. The teacher hadn't seen what actually happened, so she assumed I was the one getting too rowdy, disrupting the peace and quiet. Just as I was getting my chair back and sitting down like I should, she showed up at my desk and whacked me on the knuckles with one of those tin-edged rulers! Not only was I angry because that hurt like crazy but also because the whole thing really wasn't my fault. However, I thought it wise to let sleeping dogs lie, as we were taught to never talk back to our teachers. I'm sure the kid that caused it all was glad I kept my mouth shut.

In seventh and eighth grade, I worked on the school newspaper staff and was the editor the second year. We published a small paper once a month, perhaps four or five pages, on notebook-sized paper. The type was set by hand, and then the pages were cranked through the printing press by hand. I remember Mrs. Shaw, our English and journalism teacher, telling me that every time I got printing ink on my hands, I always ended up with it on the end of my nose as well. I'm sure she was right. Even today, if I have my hands in some kind of goo, my nose is bound to itch!

Our little grade school paper wasn't much. Usually, articles about the teachers and what subjects they were teaching at the time. And always a few articles on sports, telling about the games coming up or the ones we had won or lost. The editor always got to write an editorial, expressing his or her opinion on something relevant at the time. So in the eighth grade, that was me, and even though I won't tell you any of the subjects I wrote about, it was always fun to get to spout off about something!

In the spring of 1960, our newspaper staff went to the Oregon capitol, Salem, with an appointment to interview Governor Mark Hatfield. I still remember how nervous I was as I stood out in the rotunda, I guess waiting for our appointed time to go in. I noticed a pleasant-looking man in a very nice suit that came in the door. All the women in that area must have been expecting him because they instantly formed a big circle around him with notebooks and pieces of paper held out to be autographed. I figured, hey, this guy must be somebody if they are making such a big fuss over him, so I waded into the crowd and held out my notepad for him to sign. But try as I might, every time I got my paper in front of him, somebody would put theirs on top of mine. At one point, he looked at me and smiled as if to say he saw my dilemma, but he never got down to my paper to sign it. Finally, I figured it just wasn't worth all that bother, so I gave up. Later, someone told me he was a senator from Massachusetts, so I thought, "What the heck, what do I care about some senator from the East anyway?" As the year went by, however, that senator began to appear in the news and on TV because he had been in Salem on his campaign trail, stumping for president. To think I came so close to having an in-person autograph from John F. Kennedy! If I had only known, I'd have stepped right on some lady's head if I had to! But since I don't have the autograph, you'll just have to take my word on this one.

There was one issue of our paper that was extra special—the December issue was all about tuberculosis. I know that sounds funny now since it's pretty much extinct, but then it was a major disease. We reported everything we could find on it, the causes, the symptoms, and the remedies. The year I was editor, we won the National Tuberculosis Association award for the best coverage. Some big wigs from the association came to Lebanon and held a special dinner at which they presented the award to the teacher and newspaper staff. All I remember about that dinner is that none of us country bumpkins knew how to eat fried chicken with a knife and fork. But not to worry—one of the guys from the association must have noticed our dilemma because he immediately picked up his chicken with his fingers and started to eat! I sure hope he knew how relieved we all were.

One of the funniest things that I recall from that era happened one school evening when I had stayed after school to help set up the type and print the newspaper. It was long after school had let out but wasn't dark yet. I didn't have a way home, so Mrs. Shaw always gave me a ride. When we came out to go home, there was Mr. Ediger's (another teacher) little Volkswagen sitting in a flower bed. I found out the next day that a bunch of eighth-grade boys had picked it up and deposited it there as a joke. The only reason that was possible was the VW back then was very small and had an engine about twice the size of the one in your average washing machine. So even though it probably had more metal in it than today, it didn't weigh a lot. The next day, the joke wasn't even close to funny. It didn't take very long for the principal to determine who the culprits were, and they were called into his office pronto. I never knew what their punishment was, but the first thing they did was get Mr. Ediger's VW out of that flower bed.

I briefly mentioned one of my teachers, Mrs. Shaw. Of all the great teachers I had in school, she stands out the most in my memory. Maybe just because I spent a lot more time with her than any others, but I like to think it was more than that. Mrs. Shaw was the kind of teacher they make movies about. Words like integrity, inspiration, dedication—they all fit the image. I remember when we were back in the lower grades, the kids in junior high used to tell us, "You better hope you never get Mrs. Shaw—she's mean and eats little kids like you for breakfast," or something scary like that. So we all dreaded moving on up to the seventh and eighth grades, thinking how awful she must be. The real truth? Yes, she was tough and didn't take any guff from any of the rowdies, but it was because she really cared that each of her students went on to high school with the best education she could give them. As I mentioned before, she spent a lot of her personal time after school helping put the newspaper together then took the time to give anyone who needed it a ride home.

The most memorable thing about her, however, was something that happened at eighth grade graduation time. A lot of the kids in our school came from poor families, but there was one girl, in particular, that was worse off than the rest. She always came to school in shabby clothes, usually not very clean, and let's just say her personal hygiene wasn't the greatest either. The day before our graduation ceremony, Mrs. Shaw arranged with a few of the wealthier girls to take that girl to one of their homes. There, they allowed her to have a bath then washed and styled her hair. The next day, she came to the ceremony, decked out in a brand-new dress and shoes, all bought by Mrs. Shaw. Not that it was public knowledge that she had furnished the girl's clothes. She never told a soul. But I was the boy who walked beside that particular girl in our procession, and she told me, with tears in her eyes, how it all came about!

This item comes under the heading of "Most Humiliating Moments." When I was a junior in high school, our family doctor, Dr. Reid, had been following my progress all through school. I guess because he had been the one who saved me from heart problems when I was eight. He felt a special attachment to me. He knew I had worked on the grade school and high school newspapers and was now the editor of the latter. He was an active member of the Rotary Club in town, so he nominated me for Junior Rotarian of the month. That meant I had to go to one of their lunch meetings and give a speech, telling them how honored I was to be nominated. Well, to say I was nervous is to say the Grand Canyon is sort of a large ditch! I was never good at speaking in front of people, and these were most of the businessmen in town. I stood up, notes in hand, and proceeded to tell them how proud I was to be nominated Junior <u>Kiwanian</u> of the month! You know, someone once said you couldn't un-ring a bell—and I could not take back that one word. I just finished my speech and wished I could slither under the door on the way out. Sometimes I think I have calluses in the roof of my mouth from changing FEET!

They say there's no such thing as bad luck, but I still wonder. I graduated <u>thirteenth</u> in my class of three hundred. And to top that, my senior picture in the yearbook has a black mark right across my face! However, I did have good enough grades for a shot at some scholarships. One of them was from Crown-Zellerbach, the local paper company. My school counselor told me with my grades and the advanced classes I had completed, I was a sure thing. If I said $2,500 a year now, people would laugh and say that that wouldn't even buy all the books, but then it was just about a "full ride" at Oregon State. The problem for me was I had to fill out a lot of paperwork, including my family's financial situation. I guess it was Dad's ego or inferiority complex—whatever. He refused to give me any information about how much he made. I reminded him of the times when he said the ones that really needed it never got it and that they had no way of knowing I needed it if he didn't tell them. He refused, so the whole thing never got off the ground.

The other situation was a four-year full scholarship from First National Bank. My friend Greg and I were the top two candidates, and Greg won out. I wasn't too sure I would have liked it anyway because, after the four years of college, you had to agree to work for the bank for another four years. I met up with Greg at our ten-year class reunion—he never finished the program, either! He had the same misgivings as I did, so halfway through college, he dropped out of the program. That did make losing a bit more tolerable.

Out Standing in My Field

I started my childhood vocation of picking berries and beans at the ripe old age of six. Dad had just started at the lumber mill in 1952, and as luck would have it, the workers went on strike in the summer of 1953. My younger brother Ray had just been born in April, and Dad had no other source of income, so he had to work in the berry and bean fields that summer. Since Mom had the new baby, I had to go with Dad. I don't think I set any new records for picking that year, but the next year, since I was an experienced "field hand," I was sent out again with Pauline to work—and every summer after that until I was old enough to get an hourly job.

Every summer was the same routine—strawberries in June, raspberries in July, and pole beans in August. We would catch the work bus down at the end of our street at about 7 a.m., work until around 4:00 p.m. or 5:00 p.m., depending on how much the farmer had to get done, then ride the bus back home. This was at least five days per week and Saturday, too, if the crops required it.

I'm sure the Labor Relations Board folks would have a coronary now if they saw working conditions like ours back then, but we didn't think anything of it. It was just the way things were done everywhere. Picking was not age-discriminate. We had everyone from six years old with their parents to one guy that was in his nineties! Drinking water was brought out every morning in a large wooden keg with a spout on the front and replenished each afternoon. But you'd better not be caught hanging around the water keg when you were supposed to be picking! A few times like that and you were asked not to come back anymore. Bathrooms were just pit toilets, not the chemical outhouses like they make today, but just an outhouse sitting over a large hole, which got moved to a new hole when that got full! Once, a young picker dropped his wallet down the hole with all his punched tickets in it. Needless to say, he didn't try to get it back. You could say he was kind of like our country today—his economy was in the toilet.

Strawberry picking paid 25¢ per "carrier," which was a wooden box with a handle on top that held six of those little square berry boxes. You pushed the carrier ahead of you as you picked on your knees. I would venture a bet that I spent more time on my knees than a Catholic priest! On a good day, I might pick ten or twelve of those carriers, but some days, it was more like five or six. Each time you took one up to check it in, a person there would punch a ticket that you kept with you. Then at the end of the season, when the picking was done, you took all your punched tickets to the farmer, and he gave you a check for the season's work. My season's earnings for strawberries were usually on the order of $30 (or so).

Whatever crop you were picking, there were always several over-seers or what they called "row bosses." Their job was to walk up and down the berry or bean rows at random and check to see if you were picking all that you should be. If you were leaving too many ripe ber-ries or beans large enough to be picked, you were not "picking clean" and were sent back as far as necessary to clean up the row. Likewise, if you were picking berries too green or beans much too small, you were reprimanded, warned that such action would result in dismissal, and sometimes not paid for what you had picked incorrectly. Since most kids knew that getting fired from picking would not only result in no money at the end of summer but also usually worse discipline at home, they didn't mess up too often. Of course, you must remem-ber that the kids that were picking were of lower income, so they needed the job. All the wealthier kids were meantime lying around their swimming pools or away at Camp Run-Amok, having a good time.

In July, or thereabouts, we started raspberries. At least we were glad they were taller, so we didn't have to work on our knees! We had a different technique here, which involved a wooden box that you tied around your waist with a rope, called a "belly box," and that held two of those little berry boxes. When you filled those, you transferred them to a twelve-box crate. When the crate was full, you took it up to a checker, who again punched your ticket, and you started again with an empty crate. A crate of raspberries paid 60¢, and on a good day, I picked six to eight or when the picking wasn't so good, maybe four. The worst thing about raspberries was that when the sun got hot, they got really soft, so if you weren't careful, you could end up with a crate of mush!

One year when I was about twelve, I was working for a farmer named Dale Morris. He came to some of his better pickers and asked us if we would like to spend a day every week or so picking "black-caps," which is what we called black raspberries, for his friend and neighboring farmer. I was chosen not because I was one of the fastest pickers he had but because I was dependable. Anyway, about ten of us agreed to go. Every day, we picked for the neighbor, at lunchtime he gave us all a bottle of his homemade root beer from his cellar! Nothing ever tasted so good after a morning of working in the sun. Later in life, I have often thought it would be nice to have that recipe—or maybe it just tasted that good because it was such a rare treat. At the end of raspberry season, my check would run in the neighborhood of $40 (roughly speaking).

Raspberry picking had the disadvantage of having lots of thorns. They are not big thorns like you see on rose bushes or blackberries but tiny brittle thorns that break off when they poke into your skin. So my evening pastime during that month was sitting outside in the sun, trying to pick all the thorns out of my fingers. One of those times, I was sitting out by our big maple tree. I dropped the needle I was using, and knowing that Mom would be mad if I lost it, I started crawling around, combing through the grass and leaves to find it. I found it all right—sticking in my knee! Nothing serious, mind you, but it sure wasn't the way I had hoped for.

The best thing that could be said for raspberries, if there was any, was that the bushes grew short enough that we could see over them. That meant we could see the pickers on the other rows, so we could at least have others to talk to. One of our favorite jokes on others was this: Pauline, somewhere in the conversation, would say she had one sister and six brothers. Then at some point, I would say I had two sisters and five brothers. Invariably, the other person would say,

"But I thought you were both from the same family." Pauline, with her dry wit, would always remark, "Think about it."

Ah, yes, now it is August and time to pick pole beans! The good news is that I can make more money in a day than in raspberries. The bad news is that at the beginning of the bean season, all the beans are right at the bottom of the vines. So it was back on the knees for a few more weeks until most of the growth had moved up higher. Beans were picked into a three- or five-gallon bucket, depending on how strong you were. When the bucket was full, you had a cloth or burlap sack stashed somewhere up the row into which you poured the beans. When the sack was full or had all you could carry in it, you carried it up to the weighing scales, where an hourly worker weighed it, deducted a pound for the weight of the sack, and punched out that many pounds on your ticket. (You were lucky if it was a muddy day and there were a couple of pounds of mud stuck on the bottom!) The beans were then dumped into four-foot-square wooden boxes, all of which were loaded onto a flatbed truck in the evening and hauled to the cannery. All the years I picked, the price stayed at 2.5¢ per pound. On a good day, I picked about 200 pounds or $5 worth; a lot of days, not so much. But on a few occasions, I picked as high as 300 pounds if the picking was really great. By the time bean season was over, which was just about the beginning of school, I would have about $70 or $80 coming.

Now if you're doing the math, you're assuming that I now have $140 or thereabouts to spend on school clothes and supplies. But I forgot to mention one thing. Always at the end of each month or the end of each crop, Pauline and I would go downtown, cash our checks, and treat ourselves to something. Sometimes, it was a movie with popcorn and Coke. Sometimes, it was a trip around the circuit to Durlam's Bakery then to the drugstore for chocolate cokes then out to Barclay's Broiler south of town for a chicken dinner. Today, that would have taken most of our money, but then it was usually a few bucks. We were always careful to save most of our money to be ready for the new school year. There were other circumstances that affected how much we made, too, such as several days when we got rained out of the field and made very little and occasionally, days when we caught up with the crop and quit early. So the total at the end of summer could vary greatly.

One summer day, when Pauline and I were walking to town, we had to pass a big pine tree along Russell Drive, the paved street that went from our street up to the highway into town. As we passed the tree, I happened to look down, and there on the ground by its base was a five-dollar bill. Well, $5 then was like finding $50 now, so for a little while, we thought we were J. Paul Getty (or Bill Gates for you young'uns). Wow, did we have a great time in town that day, and it didn't cost us any of our money.

Until Pauline got old enough to leave home, I usually went out to pick with her. In strawberries, everyone had their own row, so there was no problem. And for some reason, she didn't have much problem picking raspberries, perhaps because you could see over the vines and see all the other pickers, a benefit psychologically speaking. But in pole beans, she was supposed to pick her side and I mine. For some reason, being stuck down between rows of beans that were seven feet tall must have depressed her. She would do pretty well for most of the morning hours, but as the day wore on, she would get slower and slower. Eventually, I would have to stop on my side, go over to hers, and catch her up. Many times, I would try to keep her spirits up by getting her to sing with me. We would try to sing all the words to some Buddy Holly song or harmonize an Everly Brothers tune. We weren't very good at any of them, but for a while, it would distract her enough that she would keep picking. Sooner or later, usually sooner though, she would sit down on her bucket and stop. Then when we got home that evening, she always caught heck because she let me out-pick her! After she left home, I didn't have a picking partner for raspberries and beans, so I was either assigned someone I knew, or as I got older, I could pick the row by myself.

By the time I was fifteen, my friend and lifelong school chum Dick and I had worked for Mr. Morris enough summers that he gave us a better job. We weren't sixteen and didn't have work permits, so he couldn't pay us by the hour, but it was almost as good since the going rate then was $1 per hour. He paid us $5 per day for weighing beans at the check-in scale and 50¢ per set for moving irrigation pipes. That meant that several times per day, we went to the field that wasn't being picked and moved a long string of irrigation pipes to a new location and turned it on again. He had two fields about a mile apart, so one of them was irrigated every day, about a half dozen moves a day. So for a ten-hour day, we almost made the hourly rate, and it was so much better than being down a bean row, picking for about half as much money.

To move the irrigation pipes, we had to uncouple a thirty-foot section from the rest of the string and lift one end to drain the water out using a wooden crutch about seven feet tall that held the weight of the pipe up off the bean row. Since I was much taller than Dick, I always got my end up in the air first, which meant he got several showers every day! The water was very cold, and he would cuss and scream obscenities at me, but I never tired of doing it. Thus, we moved each section down to the next dry area, connected it back together, and turned the water back on. To fertilize the beans, we had a fifty-five-gallon drum next to the pump that held chemical fertilizer containing nitrogen that was siphoned into the irrigation system. We found that if you held your hand in that water very long, it would get so cold it hurt, so we started bringing bottles of Coke out with us in the morning and putting them in the barrel to get nice and cold for later. The problem was one time, we took too long getting back to them, and they got cold enough to break the bottles! Boy, we had a real mess to clean up, but luckily, the boss never found out about it. I later got to wondering if all that chemical fertilizer in the water I dumped on Dick's head accounted for some of the goofy things he did. Up to graduation, though, he seemed about as normal as he had ever been prior to the "baptisms."

Since we were just fifteen that year, we only had bikes to get us to work. It was about six miles from my house to the fields and a mile between the fields. So by the time we rode out in the morning, rode between fields several times a day then home, we probably clocked close to twenty miles per day on bicycles. Add to that all the exercise we got weighing the bean sacks and moving heavy pipes. I was undoubtedly in the best shape that year of any time in my life, including military boot camp. We used to say we never worked so hard and had so much fun any other summer.

If we were lucky enough to get Saturday off or sometimes on Sunday when we didn't have to work, we would spend the day down on the Santiam River, swimming and trying to get a suntan all in one day. Since sunscreen was unheard of, the best we had was suntan lotion or oil, which I think was just a basting liquid so we cooked more evenly! So many times, we went home in the evening, burned so badly that we swore to ourselves we'd never be that stupid again— only to go back sometime later and do it again. Terry's (my other best school bud) mom said, at one of those times, she had a surefire remedy for a bad sunburn. She mixed baking soda and vinegar into a thin paste and smeared it all over our burned backs and shoulders. Aside from the fact that it was like rubbing an open wound with Comet cleanser, the chemical reaction would have kept a small nuclear power plant going for about a year. I just remember both of us running around and around his house, screaming at the top of our lungs. I guess I blanked out all the painful details following that. All I remember is about a month later, we were back at the river, getting sunburned again. I did manage to stay away from Terry's mom until it healed.

School Clothes

This was a ritual that always happened after the bean season was over. By that time, we had the money from all three crops that year, and it was time to go see just how far that money would go, buying our clothes for school. Since there was only one department store in Lebanon at the time, JC Penney, it didn't take a lot of gasoline or shoe leather to do the shopping. Yep, that's pretty much where most of the money was spent (except for some for food and entertainment that I mentioned earlier).

Being a typical guy, I really don't remember what Pauline bought with her money—girl stuff, of course, but what, I have no idea. For me, it was the same routine every year, three pairs of jeans, three long-sleeved shirts (flannel), packages of three T-shirts and shorts, three pairs of socks, and, of course, one pair of new leather shoes. Back then, new shoes had to be broken in, so invariably, I ended up with blisters on my heels the first week or so of school. I still remember the smell of the new leather in those shoes though. Once in a great while, I catch that smell in a store somewhere, and oh, how it takes me back! I heard someone say once that your sense of smell is the most nostalgic of all your senses, and I certainly believe it. Even the pungent odor of wild mustard weed—it's not at all a pleasant one, but it brings with it visions of the fun we used to have in the vacant lot by my house. It's not the smell itself but what it is associated with within one's mind.

How did I get from school clothes to mustard weed, anyway? Oh well, as I was saying, since Oregon is not exactly Miami Beach, I had to have a warm coat as well. That pretty much rounded out the list of clothes for school, but then there were clothes for gym class. That always chafed my hide since I was never allowed to take part in anything close to exercise in gym class, but I always had to "dress down" for it. I got the honor of bringing out the baseball gear or the basketballs or whatever the season called for—what today's kids would call the "geeky stuff." Oh yeah, and I got to keep score or fetch the towels, whatever the PE teacher asked me to do. The teachers apparently thought it was better for me to be a part of the class than not, but it was pretty much just humiliating! But I've digressed again…where was I?

Okay, gym clothes. That was easy, just some more underwear, white T-shirts, socks, gym shorts of the appropriate color, and tennis shoes. Nowadays, you can get tennis shoes in about two hundred styles and colors, ranging in price from a few hundred to a few thousand dollars, or so I'm told. But at the Penney's store, there was one and only one style—black-and-white high-tops. Yes, I know those are popular with the kids now, but when I was buying them, they were just the only thing available, and boy, were they ugly! By the time I was in high school, we were all rescued from our ugliness when Converse came out with their low-cut version. That immediately became the shoe to be seen in or to wear to the gym, so if you didn't have those, you just weren't "in." The drawback to all this was that the new Converse sold for a whopping $5, whereas you could buy Penney's generic shoe for only $2.98. Not a big difference, you say? Well, it was when you had to watch every penny to make sure you got everything you NEEDED—"need" being the operative word. And you had to allot some of the money for school supplies too. So when they first came out, I didn't get to wear the cool tennies, but after I started working by the hour at the gas station, you can bet I never wore any other kind—with tall white crew socks and jeans that were tapered or "pegged" at the bottom, short enough that a few inches of sock always showed. After all, image is everything in school, right?

Rheumatic Fever

There was only one summer growing up that I got out of picking crops. That was the summer of 1955 when I was eight. On May 10 of that year, a day that will live in my mind all my life, I was home from school with what I thought was a sprained ankle. Since I had had a scuffle with Johnny Arts next door a few days before, I blamed it on that. But the day before, I had been home with what I thought was the same problem. Mom was more astute than I and caught the fact that the second day, I was complaining with a different ankle than the day before! So, of course, her first thought was that I was faking to get out of going to school. Lucky for me, my brother Jim was home on leave from the Army at the time, and as he said later, he just thought I didn't look well. So he hauled me uptown to Dr. Reid's office for a checkup. The doc said when he came in to listen to my heart that he could hear the gurgling sound with his stethoscope even before he touched my chest. The heart murmur was apparently that bad. He told Jim to take me home, put me in bed, and not to let me get out again. He said I had rheumatic fever, a condition in which the bacterium streptococcus (the same one that causes strep throat) not only attacks the heart valves, resulting in a severe heart murmur but also causes inflammation of the joints, hence the "sprained ankle." It was only by a sheer miracle that Jim was there to take me to the doctor. Otherwise, I guess Mom would have sent me on to school, thinking nothing was really wrong with me.

That was the start of my whole summer confined to bed. The first month or so, the doctor came out a couple of times per week to give me a shot of bicillin, some kind of powerful antibiotic of that time. Once, he tried to get a blood test from me, but that was apparently not his forte, and he managed to stick one arm a half dozen times then the other arm several times before he successfully hit a vein. By that time, I was ready to wolf my cookies all over him. After that, he sent a lab technician from the hospital out to do the deed, for which I was truly thankful.

As much as I dreaded going out to pick berries and beans every year, I found, while lying inert in my prison cell, that I was longing to get up and go pick! Anything was better than being eight years old and confined to bed. Now I know this will shock some people, but remember, times were different, and a lot of the blood-borne diseases of today weren't known. One of the times, Dr. Reid came out to shoot his wonder drug into my backside. He gave me the needle and syringe and told my mom to get me a bowl of water. He then told me that anytime one of the neighbor kids went by the screened window, I should draw that syringe full of water and squirt them through the screen! Well, I had a great time doing that for a while until let's see, I either got tired of it, or too many of my victims threatened to kill me. I finally had to cease-fire. I kept that needle and syringe in a box of junk that kids keep, along with my petrified frog, wooden yoyo, and Captain Midnight decoder ring, just to remind me of the dedication our family doctor had—how he had sympathized with me and tried to make my confinement more bearable.

From May 10, I was confined to bed until sometime in late September or October. I was supposed to start the third grade that year, so my teacher, Mrs. Link, came to my house every week to bring my schoolwork. So I thought, "Darn, I'm too sick to get out of bed but well enough to still have to do my homework?" Faithful she was, too, and brought that work every single week, as well as picking up and grading what I had done before. So when I was able to get up and go back to school, I was not behind the others in my class. I was just shorted one summer. Five months in bed! What a bummer that was!

I think I mentioned before that a year or so before this occurred, Dad had bought us a black-and-white TV. So during my forced incarceration all that summer, someone would pick me up and move me from my bed in the front bedroom to the living room couch, where I could watch TV. (Would you believe General Hospital was on, even back then?) I know Pauline felt sorry for me in one way, but another part of her teenage brain was jealous! I had no external signs of injury or disease, and yet I got to lie in bed all day, every day, while she still had to go out to pick berries and beans. One day, as I lay on that couch, we got into a pretty heated argument about something or possibly nothing. Before I realized what I was doing, I jumped up and tried to run after her. The only problem was that my legs and feet had not felt the weight of my body, skinny though it was, for several months. As soon as I stood up to run, I fell flat on my face! She must have really felt guilty about that because she quickly scooped me up and deposited my carcass back on the couch—before Mom had time to see what happened.

For several years after all that, I went to the doctor's office one Saturday of every month and got shot in the rear again. I don't know if that regimen would be accepted in today's medical world, but all I know is that when I got my draft notice at age nineteen, the Army doc's in Portland couldn't find a sign of a heart murmur. They classified me 1-A—eligible to be drafted, which they did. Of course, you must realize, about that time during the war, they would draft you if you could walk upright and breathe without assistance.

Fishing

Fishing was one of only two things we boys did with Dad—the other was hunting. And he didn't consider us ready for either one until we were about twelve—well, maybe a bit younger for fishing—but you had to be twelve in Oregon to hunt deer, and that's the only thing he hunted when I was at home. So when he finally decided that I was old enough to go with the rest of the family, I got to make the long, nauseating trip to the coast, usually Newport, with them. If you make the trip from Lebanon to Newport now, the highway is pretty straight, and it takes about an hour. But in the '50s, Highway 20 was a slow, windy road that had so many hairpins turns in it that it took us at least two hours. Dad used to say the turns were so sharp you could meet yourself coming back! Every time we made the trip, I got car sick. It really doesn't make a fishing trip more fun if you are already sick before you even get in the boat.

Sometimes, we fished in Yaquina Bay, but we didn't own a boat. Dad had bought a small outboard motor, however, so we would go to one of the marinas, rent a small fishing boat, and put Dad's motor on it. Now, by small, I don't mean it would only sleep a dozen people aboard. It was more like, if you had more than four people in it, someone was sitting on someone else's lap, and the boat was probably sinking. Most of them were on the order of 12 feet long. Moreover, the seats were just two metal or wooden benches across the width of the boat with a single in the back for the guy who ran the motor. Since we always got there at Dawn Minus 30, they were most always wet. We never seemed to remember anything to dry them off with, except the seats of our pants, so there, we sat for the next eight hours or so on a hard bench seat in wet pants! I won't say exactly what my older brothers liked to call the condition, but it was their version of "plank-butt." As if sitting down on those seats all day with your knees up under your chin wasn't enough, then your rear got to itching, and if you squirmed too much, you rocked the boat and incurred the Wrath of Ike since Dad did not like squirmy kids.

One day, when we were on the bay, Wayne caught something he didn't know what to do with. We always used a big chunk of white clam meat on a very large hook and 4 or 5 ounces of weight to hold the hook still in the tide current. So after baiting his hook, he gave the whole mess a big heave-ho to get lots of lines out. As that bait and sinker were tracing their arc across the sky, a seagull spotted what he thought was instant dinner. Swooping down, he grabbed the clam bait in midair and started to fly away! Well, this was not like anything we had caught before, so Wayne just kept playing that seagull back and forth, back and forth, while he continued to reel it closer and closer to the boat. He later said he was going to get the bird as close as possible then cut his line, assuming the gull had swallowed the clam. Bringing the bird on board was not an option since gulls are big enough and mean enough to take off your finger with one bite. As it happened, when he got the seagull up close to the boat, the bird dropped the bait and flew off. But not until all the other fishermen in a half dozen boats had a good laugh at his expense.

Other times, if the adults decided, we didn't go out on the bay but fished off the North Jetty, a jetty being a long finger of rock jutting out into the ocean made by man to create a wind and water-break at the entrance to the bay. There was also a South Jetty, but for some reason, we never fished there. To get out to where we fished, you had to walk and carry all your gear for about a half mile then hop and skip down over some really big boulders to get close enough to the water to fish. We mostly fished on the bayside of the jetty since that's where we found the catching to be the best. In those days, we could, with some exceptions, count on taking home a large gunny sack of flounder, sole, and even several Dungeness crabs. The crabs would grab onto the piece of clam we used for bait and didn't want to let go. Since the clam meat was very tough, we could pull the crab right up to the top of the water then quickly yank them onto a rock. Then into a separate sack, they went as long as they were large enough to be legal. We didn't know at the time that all three of those were very expensive to buy in the store. The downside of fishing on that side of the jetty was the cold wind. It almost always came out the southwest, which meant we were right in its path. Sometimes, we would get so cold you couldn't tell if what you stuck on your hook was a piece of clam or your finger. So we would take a break, go over to the other side, where there was no wind, and sit in the sun until we thawed out, so to speak. Or, if you were lucky, you might find a small nook behind a large rock where you could still hold your rod but be out of the wind. One time, when I found such a sheltered cove, I got a little too comfortable and dozed off. Well, brother Jim being a born joker, he could not pass up an opportunity like that, so from up above me, he took a long piece of driftwood and gave my pole a good hearty whack! I came awake, thinking, of course, that I had hooked a small orca and gave such a jerk that any fish on the other end would have been gutted instantly anyway. Oh, what a horse laugh he got from that one! But I learned from that to guard my fishing pole if I intended to take a nap.

Speaking of Jim and his jokes, he was one of those people that never gave anyone a straight answer if he could help it. One day, on the way back to the car, we had caught so many fish. One person could not easily carry the sack. So Jim and our friend Andy had tied the top then stuck a large stick through the top so they could both carry it. An unsuspecting victim, walking in the opposite direction on the jetty, never imagining that anyone could catch that many fish, asked innocently what they had in the sack. Of course, Jim couldn't pass up the opportunity and replied, "It's our other buddy. He died out there fishing," then just kept on walking. The look on those people's faces was priceless. If that were today, I'm sure one of them would whip out a cell phone and dial 911.

Uncle Roy, who was with us on many of our trips to the coast, once caught the biggest, ugliest thing any of us had ever seen. He hauled it in, thinking he had a large flounder, many of which would go 2 feet long and weigh 4 or 5 pounds. But when he pulled it up onto a large flat rock, there was this dark, blackish-green monster, about 3 feet long with a head about twice the diameter of his body, and rows of the sharpest-looking teeth anyone could imagine. None of us had ever seen one before, so he was not sure just what he should do with it. A veteran fisherman of the area happened to be walking by on top of the jetty and yelled down that it was a wolf eel. He tossed down a large stick of driftwood and told my uncle to kill it before he dumped it back into the ocean since they were known to ravage the fish population. Uncle Roy said that the thing was so mean-looking, he was even afraid to get close enough to club it to death! But club it he did and quickly disposed of it into the water.

I fished with the family on the coast for all the years until I left home for the military and had the pleasure of catching many, many large fish. Years after I left, I was told that the good fishing ended in Yaquina Bay due to a large herd of sea lions moving in and eating up all the fish. Wayne, Jim, and some others continued to go out into the ocean and drift fish along the coast in that area but never again was the fishing in the bay like it was back then.

A lot of our fishing trips were not to the coast but to some of the many lakes and reservoirs in Oregon. I can remember many fun trips to places like Detroit Lake, Prineville Reservoir in central Oregon, or several other places we loved to go. On one particular trip to Prineville, Dad and I came back into camp with both of our limits of trout, the personal limit then being ten. Yes, we had twenty nice fish, all right, but as he loved to tell for years after that, he had caught seventeen of them, and I caught the other three! So—what? I said I had done a lot of fishing. I never said I did a lot of catching! His gloating on that trip was short-lived, however. A sudden rainstorm caused a small flash flood that ran under our tent and soaked everything we had, so we had to pack up and go home.

Hunting

Arriving at the age of hunting to me was a rite of passage. At age twelve, I was allowed by the state to take my hunter's safety course and buy my hunting license and deer tag. That was a big deal to me since, as I have said before, Dad didn't play golf or Monopoly or anything else with us, so to finally get to go hunting with him, my brothers, and Uncle Roy was a real step up. We never hunted anything but deer as long as I was home, although after I left, Dad did take up hunting elk. And that was only because, on his very first elk hunting trip, he shot a six-point bull right beside the road. They didn't even have to drag it to the truck! Anyway, that hooked him on hunting elk. The bad news is that he never even got another shot at one in all the years after that.

As a matter of fact, that thing with the elk is very similar to how our family started hunting deer. Shortly after moving to McKinney Lane, Bob made friends with another local boy whose family hunted, so Bob bought a license and deer tag and went out with them. By ten o'clock that morning, he was back with his deer. Of course, then everyone thought this was like shooting the proverbial fish in a barrel, so they went downtown and got Dad a license and tag. Before the day was out, Dad also had a deer! That hooked my family on deer hunting. They thought this had to be the easiest and cheapest meat ever. More bad news—that never happened again. Oh, the time and money that was spent over the next several decades, trying to bag that buck, or as a last resort, even a doe. We even laughed many times at how much a deer was going to cost per pound if we did happen to shoot one. By the time all the necessary tags and licenses, guns and ammunition, camping gear, appropriate hunting apparel, gas and accessories for the trucks were bought, I'm sure the cost must have been in the hundreds of dollars per pound some years. But then, that didn't take into account all the fun we had trying. There were not many things that could compare with a day out with all the guys, hoping for that big buck to step out right where you wanted him.

One year we had a special treat. To balance the deer herds, the state decided to issue special tags for a single weekend in December, for bucks only. Well, as luck would have it, on Thanksgiving Day, about two weeks before that, Dad developed appendicitis and had to have it removed. So when the weekend of the hunt came, he was still not getting around as he usually did and wasn't supposed to lift much for a while. By midafternoon, the other two guys and I already had a buck in the back of the pickup, so we were all three standing by it, probably enjoying a cup of coffee after a hard day of tramping through brush and canyons. Just as we saw Dad coming slowly up the logging road we were on, a nice buck came up over the embankment below us, ran right past us, and up the hill, looking like he'd already been shot at. All three of us had to scramble for our rifles, but we did manage to get off a few shots in the general direction of the deer, thinking, of course, that since Dad was not at his peak, we could help him out. But no good deed goes unpunished, as they say, especially when the deed is illegal! Shooting at any game after your bag limit is filled is strictly that—illegal, I mean. Since Murphy's Law usually applies, the game warden that we all affectionately called Sergeant York was on duty, watching our every move from up around the bend. It only took him a minute or so to get down to where we were and issue all three of us citations. Later on, I found out that it cost the other two guys a $50 fine since they were adults. Now that doesn't sound like much, but then it was about half a week's pay. For me, since I was only fourteen at the time, I got a visit at our house from a state-appointed counselor, who gave me a long lecture about breaking the law. But at the time, it didn't seem like the wrong thing. We had good intentions, and besides, we only had a split second to think about it. When a big buck almost runs over you, the normal thing to do is SHOOT!

Dad, for all his extra years on me, was a tough old guy and hard to keep up with hunting. He had grown up farming then working years in a lumber mill, and all I was in my early teens was a wimpy, skinny kid that hadn't been afforded the opportunity to get in shape due to my bout with rheumatic fever at age eight. Even though this was years later, I had not been allowed to take part in school PE or do any strenuous exercise. So as you might see, I wasn't very tough. Not only that, but I have never been very coordinated. One day, while trying to keep up with that old water buffalo, he decided to walk right on across a log that spanned a small creek. Sensing that I was not right behind him, he turned to find me stopped, just looking with terror at that small slick wet log! I knew even before I stepped out that I, having the grace of a three-legged hippo on a railroad trestle, would never get all the way across without falling off. Now if you were to put a 2×4 board flat on the ground, I could probably walk it for a way but put a twelve-inch log up about 10 feet over a running creek, and forget it, Alice! At that, he got quite irritated and told me in no uncertain terms to get on that log and come on across. Finally, I did so, and by some miracle, I made it without falling off—only because the one thing I had more fear of than falling off that log was Dad's anger. I knew sooner or later, I'd have to face him, and if I didn't get across somehow, it was not going to be a pretty sight. I couldn't hear for sure what he said after that as he went on ahead, mumbling, I think, something about how in the world he got such a gangly, clumsy kid! I'm sure he meant it in the nicest way though.

I think the most fun I had in all the years I hunted with our family and friends was the one-week trip we made to Central Oregon. Since hunting season was always in October, I got to take a whole week out of school for the trip, which made it even better. But in those days, it wasn't free. In the weeks before, you had to do all that week's lessons ahead of time and get them turned in before they would allow you a week off. So I did, and off we went. I don't know exactly why, but I learned to love that high flat desert where we went so much more than the western area where we lived. I think it was because it was so open, not thick brush and steep canyons everywhere. For whatever reason, I never got over preferring the central part of the state and always said after I left that if I ever moved back to Oregon, it would be to that part. There was one other factor too, and that was the fact that I learned to hate the constant rain of our area, and Central Oregon had more sunny days and more likely some snow in winter instead of that incessant raining! When people say that suntan lotion in Oregon is WD-40, they're talking specifically about the western part! I don't even remember whether we tagged any deer on that trip or not. It didn't matter because I loved just being there, camping out in the open, being part of the hunting party.

Trips Back to Texas

During the summers of the years, I was ten and thirteen, Dad took his two-week vacation from the mill, and we made the trip back to Texas and Oklahoma. In Texas lived all of Mom's brothers and sisters. My older sister Gladys and family lived in northeastern Oklahoma. I think I mentioned it earlier, but just in case you missed it, Mom was from a family of twelve kids, the first six from her mother and another six from her stepmother. According to Mom, her mother died when Mom was only nine, and she was one of the oldest kids at the time. As a lot of men did in those times, her dad then remarried to a much younger woman, not much older than Mom's older sister. By this woman, her dad had six more kids.

So you can see, when we made the trip back to Texas, we had a lot of relatives visiting to do—which was all we did. I guess it's a good thing Dad was an only child; otherwise, we'd have needed another week! Most of them lived in the western part of Texas or up in what is called the panhandle somewhere near Amarillo. The first time, when I was ten, I was at an age where I really didn't feel very comfortable visiting people I didn't know. But the good news for me was that we didn't have time to spend more than a day with any one of them, and some of them we saw in a group, so I could tolerate that. By the time I was thirteen on the second trip, I was a little more sociable, plus I had the prior trip to get somewhat acquainted with everyone.

On the way down there the first time, I had a rude awakening at one of the rest stops. We had traveled what seemed an eternity without a stop, so when we did, I jumped out of the car and headed for the bathroom. No, I didn't even bother to put on my shoes—it was summertime, so I didn't think I needed them. I started to run across a green area I thought was a lawn, but about halfway across, I realized

75

I was walking on a bed of sharp nails! I was learning the hard way of a low-growing ground cover called goat heads. The plant does well with very little water and stays nice and green to the eye but grows a small head with two sharp thorns pointing upward, looking very much like a tiny horned goat. Well, there I was, out in the middle, so the only thing I could do was go back or keep on. Either of which was going to be more pain. I opted to go on and take care of my other urgent problem. Back at the car, Mom had her usual remedy— Merthiolate! I didn't know if she was doctoring the holes in my soles or setting my feet on fire.

The thing I liked the least about going to the south was the heat and humidity. If I were to go there now, all the houses and cars have air-conditioning, not so back then. Since I grew up in Oregon, where the air is pretty dry, it was very uncomfortable riding in a car or trying to sleep at night in their houses, where the temperature was too hot and the humidity way too high. There was one thing that helped, though, and that was the fact that when we got there, we had just spent three days non-stop in the car, so we were so beat. I probably could have slept on a bed of nails with a rock for a pillow.

There was one break on the first trip, but it wasn't because we wanted to. We were traveling in a 1949 Studebaker Champion, which had a small six-cylinder engine and not very much power. By the time we crawled all the way up to the summit of the Rocky Mountains, to what they called the Continental Divide, the engine was so hot that Dad had to stop whether he liked it or not to let it cool down. Once he turned the engine off, it was so hot that something they called "vapor lock" occurred, which meant the motor was so hot. The fuel was vaporizing before it got through the carburetor, so the engine wouldn't start. That suited Pauline and me just fine because there at Monarch Crest, there was civilization, and we got a chance to look around and get out of the car for a couple of hours.

Even though most of the trip across Idaho on US Highway 20 and 30 was just desert, some innovative businessman had found a way to make the drive more enjoyable. He apparently owned a chain of gas stations called Fearless Farris' Stinker Stations, and he had put up funny signs all across the state. I can only remember a few, one of them being at a place where there were these large, perfectly round rocks all over the ground on either side of the highway. The sign read, "Idaho watermelons—take one home to your mother-in-law." Another one said, "Idaho natives prohibited from scalping tourists within 50 feet of roadway." I don't think his definition of "scalping" was the one they use at the ballparks! They still have Stinker Stations in southern Idaho, but they are owned by Sinclair. I can't seem to find out what happened to old Fearless.

Just about all of Mom's siblings had at least one child, and some had several, which made the visit much more tolerable than having to sit and listen to the adults talk all day. At one aunt's house in Amarillo, her son Butch had planned a "campout" in his backyard with a couple of his friends, so I got to sleep outside in a sleeping bag with them. That was a lot of fun since there was a lot more joke telling and goofing off than sleeping! Butch's Texas drawl drove me nuts, though, 'cause it seemed to me he took forever to get through a joke to the punchline (diiiiidja evvvvverrrr heeaarrr the onnnne abbb-bouttttt...). On the other hand, he kept telling me to slow down, that I talked so fast he couldn't understand me. Aside from the language barrier, we got along fine, and it was a great experience for me.

One of the uncles lived out in a little house in the country, pretty much in the middle of nowhere, with nothing around but plowed ground. Needless to say, they were farmers, either for themselves or working the fields for someone else. On the day we arrived, one of his sons came home from driving a tractor all day with a story that raised the hair on my neck. It seems that in plowing a new field, the grass had built up on the plows, so he got off the tractor with a claw hammer in his hand to knock the clumps of grass loose. As he was walking back to the plow, the hammer slipped out of his hand, flying out in front of him, and landed right on top of a large coiled-up rattlesnake! This did not make the snake exactly happy, so it began to rattle like crazy. He had apparently destroyed its den as he plowed over it, but if it had not been for dropping the hammer, he would have stepped right on it and would likely have been bitten. Coming from an area of the country where we didn't ever see rattlesnakes, that sure didn't make me any fonder of rural Texas, let me tell ya!

I know you're not supposed to have favorite relatives, but I'm sure everyone does—a special person who stands out in your memory for some reason or other. In this case, that would have been my uncle and his family in Canadian, Texas. They lived in a big house with large, covered porches front and back. And on the back porch was a small refrigerator that was always full of cold soft drinks, which was pretty awesome in my book—a cold drink at your fingertips anytime you wanted it. My uncle managed his father-in-law's wheat and cattle ranches in the area, worked full time as a lineman for the electric company, and served when needed as a volunteer fireman. He was one of those people who seemed to love life and always managed to show us a good time when we were there, even though I wonder now how he had the time!

Uncle Buster had two children, a girl a couple of years older than I and a son just about my age. On the second visit to their house, we were there on the Fourth of July. After we had spent most of the morning at the public swimming pool (a rare treat in itself), my uncle gave his kids some money and told them to take me with them into town to buy some fireworks. In Texas at that time, you could buy all sorts of cool fireworks, including Black Cat firecrackers. That was unheard of in Oregon, where most fireworks were illegal. Even though this was all just old hat to them—something they did every year on the Fourth—I was pretty psyched about the whole thing. You could set off just about anything you wanted and blow up about anything as long as you did it outside the city limits. So out to the desert we went! We would drill holes in the soft sandy soil, fill them with all sorts of explosives, stand back, and watch as it blew great craters in the earth. Actually, they probably weren't that huge, but it was all new fun for me.

Oh, but I almost forgot one very unpleasant experience during our visit to Canadian. When we first arrived, my cousin was at the park, playing in a baseball game. I wanted to get to where I could see everything, so I waded through some tall green grass to the back side of the backstop. I stood there for the remainder of his game, pleased with the great spot I had to watch. By the time he and I had walked a short distance home, however, I was not so pleased as I was itching furiously from my ankles up to my knees. He, of course, told his mom about it right away. She just laughed and gave me some ointment of some kind to put on, which, after a while, stopped the itching. It seems there is a red spider, so minute that you can only see it with a magnifying glass, that lives in lush-green grassy areas of the south called a chigger. If they get on you, they burrow into your skin, much like a tick, and live off your blood. They cause you to itch like crazy, but by putting that ointment on, it smothers the chigger and soothes the itch. So I thought to myself, there's the humidity, the rattlesnakes, goat-heads, chiggers, and…what else? It seemed to me that Texas was a good place to be FROM!

After our stay in Canadian, our next stop was my sister Gladys's house in Barnsdall, Oklahoma. Since she lived up in the northeastern corner of the state, it took most of another day's driving to get there. We always spent three days or so in Barnsdall, not that it would take that long to see the town but just to visit with her family. At the time, I wasn't familiar with *The Andy Griffith Show*, but later on, when I saw the town of Mayberry on TV, I had to laugh. The show could have been filmed in Barnsdall! One day, when my nephew David and I walked up to their main street, their only town cop was sitting at the curb with his door open and his feet propped up on the open window. A few years later, I saw an episode on TV where Andy, the local sheriff, was in that very same position.

There was one very distinctive feature about the town of Barnsdall—it had an honest-to-goodness, producing OIL WELL right in the middle of Main Street! Yes, sir, right smack dab in the middle of the street was this big horse's head or whatever they call those things, bobbing up and down, pumping oil out of the ground. I never thought to ask at the time but wondered later—where was the oil going that was coming up out of the ground? Anyway, it was unique enough to be put on the local postcards and a real tourist attraction.

Gladys has always said she would never live in California because of "all those earthquakes." And yet, she lived in an area that is very often the target of tornadoes. On one visit to their house, one such tornado had come and gone not too long before. Luckily, it did not hit their house, but just down the street a couple of blocks, it had ripped the whole roof off a house on one side of the street and set it very neatly on top of the roof of the house just across the street from it! I don't know how that kind of thing happens since I would think once it sucked something up, it would whisk it away into the air. But tornadoes are known to do some very strange things. In one of the museums in their area, they have a section of a telephone pole with a piece of straw stuck completely through it—figure that out on your computer! I have always given Gladys a bad time about that since she is probably more likely to be hit by a tornado than I was to suffer damage from an earthquake while living in California. Earthquakes were the least of my worries.

One of Gladys's neighbors had a little Shetland pony, which, of course, was the delight of all the little kids, including my brother Ray, who was about seven years old on our second visit. By that time, I was thirteen, so I was too big to ride him, but I could help all the smaller kids take a ride. What we didn't know at first was, number one, Shetland ponies like to bite! More than once, we had to slap that silly thing on the nose for trying to bite one of the kids. The other thing we found out the hard way was their dirt and sweat could really cause an infection when rubbed into a mosquito bite. Ray had a bite on the inside of his wrist, so after he had been on and off the pony all day, he had managed to rub that bite on the pony's hair quite a few times. Well, by the next day, his little bite was a big red sore with a red streak running up his arm. That meant there was already an infection going up his arm, so he was rushed off to the local doctor, who gave him a shot to stop it. Naturally, that was the end of his cowboy days. Come to think of it, I don't think he ever took to horses much after that.

There were many fun sites to see around Barnsdall. Not too long a drive from them was the Will Rogers Museum and Park, which had so many great things to see inside—airplanes, American Indian displays, and a large herd of buffalo in the park. I was never a museum kind of kid, but I sure was impressed with the buffalo! And they had the world's largest wax plant right in their own town. We couldn't tour that one, but Gladys's husband Charlie worked there all the years until retirement, and he used to tell us about all the gazillion kinds of wax they produced—from common uses for candles to wax that almost all canneries of fruits and vegetables used to line the inside of the metal cans, so the contents would not react with the metal. I was told they made more kinds of wax for more different uses than any other plant in the world.

Probably the most memorable thing about our stay in Oklahoma was going fishing. The evening before we were to go, Charlie would water his front lawn down real wet then use an electric rod he had fashioned. He stuck it into the wet ground, turned it on, and presto! Up came big fat night crawlers! I've never seen that method used before or since, but it sure worked for him. After dark, we would take those crawlers and our fishing gear down to the local creek to catch catfish. The catching of the fish was fun, but looking out across the creek by the light of the lanterns and seeing water moccasins slithering across the water wasn't so fun. One night, I was sitting on a lawn chair with my bare feet sticking out toward a strip of tall grass between me and the water's edge. Suddenly, I saw that tall grass wiggle! I pulled my feet back a bit, and the grass moved again. It took me about two seconds to fit all of me, feet and all, up on that little chair, where I stayed. I could take the kidding I got from Charlie and the others better than any snake. Oh yes, and that creek? Well, years later, they dammed it up and made a really nice recreational lake there. They called it "Lake Waxoma" after that wax plant I mentioned.

Once the two or three days were spent in Barnsdall, it was time for that long boring three-day trip back to Oregon. As I said, Dad only had two weeks' vacation to do all this, so I know it wasn't his fault that we had to try to go nonstop. Sometimes, he would get so tired, he would pull over, take a short nap, then on we'd go. One time, he waited just a bit too long and drifted off the highway onto the gravel shoulder. Luckily, the noise of the gravel woke him up just in time since it was hot, and all the windows were down. I still remember looking over the edge for just an instant, though, and thinking that was a long way to fall! Dad used to say that his vacation was TWO weeks, after which you were TOO tired to go back to work, but TOO broke not TO. Later in life, I understood just what he meant.

My Friends

Our neighborhood out in the suburbs south of town was not one of the finer areas of Lebanon. Consequently, a lot of the kids that lived around me were not the kind you would want to hang around with. But, as in the worst of neighborhoods, there are always a few good ones. I knew all the bad kids because we all went to the same school, and I knew a lot of reasons to steer clear of them. Luckily, I was in the same grade with Terry and Dick, who became my two best friends through all our years of school.

Terry lived on Russell Drive, about two-thirds of the way to the main highway from my house. His family, that being just his folks, him, and a younger brother Mike lived in a two-story house, which was always a fascination to me in those days, and I used to think, when I got my own house, it would be two-story. Anyway, Terry had a bedroom all to himself upstairs, so he had more privacy than I did. Not only did I share my room with Ray, but it was only a window away from the living room, so everything we said could be heard by all. We spent many, many hours just hanging out in Terry's room, playing records on his record player, and probably trying to sing along with most of them. In those days, of course, there were no computers, iPods, or cell phones, and very few families had more than one TV—the one in their living room. That made his little record player a very valuable commodity.

Terry's brother Mike, whom we called Mikey, was two or three years younger, so he was seldom included in the gang. Ray was six years younger than I, so he was too far behind in age to want to hang out with us. I used to tell people that I was an only child from a family of eight kids! Because Pauline was five years older and Ray was six years younger, I was never as close to any of my siblings as I would have liked to have been.

Dick lived sort of south of Terry, over by the highway but a few blocks from it, behind the old Pine Lodge grocery store. It was probably about the same distance from his house to Terry's as it was from mine, so we all lived within easy walking distance of each other. Dick was smaller in stature than Terry and I, as well as being over a year younger, even though we were all in the same grade. Not only was he born in an earlier month, but he also started school back in Missouri or one of those foreign places where they let kids start school at age six. All that to say because he was smaller and knew he was younger than we were, he was always trying to prove himself. Mom always called guys like that "Bantie Roosters," a southern corruption of Bantam, which was a small variety of chickens. Nowadays, I guess they just call it a "small-man complex." Anyway, although we never thought of him as any less than we were, he always had to fight harder, swim farther, and play sports better than anyone else.

I'll always believe the real reason for Dick's complex was that he was adopted at a very young age and moved to Oregon. We never really knew for sure what happened to his parents since, over the years, we heard conflicting stories. One story was that they died in a car wreck. But for whatever reason, he and his older sister were adopted by an older couple, neither of whom seemed to me to want kids. I often wondered why his parents took in two young kids. I didn't see too much of his dad, but his mom seemed very strict and cold. Every time I had occasion to be at Dick's house, I always went away with a sigh of relief to be gone. I can't put my finger on the reason. It was just a feeling that there was very little love in that home.

There was one thing that Dick was really good at, at which none of the rest of us could even compete. He had played drums for the school band since way back in grade school, so by the time we were in high school, he was very good. He played not only for the large band but also for the pep band, which played popular music for school functions, such as special assemblies or dances. I always thought he would go far in the world as a drummer, but once we graduated, I don't know any more about him.

Most of those hours we three spent in Terry's room were winter hours since there was much to do outside in good weather. Down by Cascade Plywood mill, about a quarter mile from my house, there was a thick patch of timber. The whole thing was probably not more than five acres, but to us, it was a million miles from civilization. The trees were all huge and so thick. There was very little undergrowth. You could see all around under them, and it was always dark and cool, even in the summertime, the ground being a thick, soft carpet of fir needles. We would use dead limbs to build a frame then cover it with fir boughs to make a hideout or a remote mountain cabin or an Indian tepee, depending on where our imagination took us that day. Back then, it wasn't about a lot of expensive store-bought toys. It was about the excitement to see what we could dream up then scrape up to make up whatever we had thought up. It's amazing to see what a kid can do with just his or her imagination and a cardboard box!

One of those days in our woods, we had brought along some hot dogs and built a small bonfire to roast them (kids, don't try this at home). Dick was sent out to cut some sticks to put the hot dogs on, and he came back with three of the straightest, nicest roasting sticks we had ever seen. What I didn't know until later that day was that Dick was not allergic to it, so those sticks were poison oak with all the limbs and leaves removed. There was no way I could have identified them, so here I was, not only handling the stick but also eating a hot dog that had been on the stick! That was about midday, and by bedtime that night, I was already breaking out with poison oak rash all over my hands, arms, face, and even inside my mouth. And by the next day, I pretty much had the stuff all over my body. It finally got so bad that my ears and eyes swelled shut, and I had to go to the doctor for a cortisone shot. In all the hundred or so times I've had poison oak, that's the only time I've ever been that bad. Dick felt bad about it for a little while, but once I recovered, it was a big joke that I had caught it, and he hadn't.

Then there was the river. Just a couple of miles to the east, down Russell Drive, past the city canal, then on down the river road was the Santiam River. Even in the summertime, the water in that river was ice cold. But to a bunch of kids, it didn't matter, and if we had a day off that was hot, that's where we'd be. There was what was called a diversion dam (to divert water into the local canal for city water) on the river there, which was only about 10 feet high, but it was enough to back the river up into a slower-moving lakelike area. And that's where we went to swim and get sunburned. A lot of the time, we weren't actually swimming but floating. Up on the highway from our houses, there was a tire shop where you could get used car and truck inner tubes, patch the holes in them, and use them on the river as floaty toys. (For those of you who are too young to know, tubeless car tires weren't that common.) Or sometimes, we would float down a stretch of the city canal on the tubes, even though we weren't supposed to be in it or on it at all. Oh, if I only had a buck for every time, I came home with a big red scratch up my back or stomach from trying to jump into the inner tube and have the valve stem scrape me as I went through. But that never seemed to stop us from doing it again the first chance we got.

Then there was the occasional fishing trip the three of us went on. One particular Saturday, we decided we would go over to a slough that was just off the Willamette River and spend the night camping out and fishing. Now we didn't exactly plan this trip out the way we should have, so there were some things left behind that we were to need that night. For instance, once we caught some fish, we had a skillet, but we didn't bother to take any kind of oil in which to cook them! So we tried the alternative method—fry them in water! Obviously, that didn't work at all since we ended up with a panful of boiled fish parts, looking somewhat like a poor man's fish stew. I wondered in later years why we didn't just put each fish on a stick and roast it over the fire. I hear poison-oak branches make great skewers!

I guess you might say it was Terry's fault that I started smoking on a regular basis. Just kidding! But his house was the one place we could get cigarettes without getting caught. When I first started trying to smoke, my dad was the only one in our house that smoked, and he always knew exactly how many packs of cigarettes he had. So that ruled out trying to borrow any of his. But at Terry's, both his mom and dad smoked, and they always had a kitchen drawer full of cigarettes. Since they both smoked, neither of them ever knew how many packs were in the drawer, so it was easy to borrow a pack now and then. The unfortunate part of all this was that they smoked unfiltered Camels, a cigarette that would bring the Incredible Hulk to his knees! But we were determined to overcome that hurdle and finally learned to smoke them. Later, when I could buy my own, I switched to another unfiltered brand, Lucky Strikes, which were just as bad. When Wayne got out of the Navy and moved back home, he talked me into switching to his brand, Pall Mall. Before long, I realized that it was so he could borrow cigarettes from ME! I guess what goes around comes around. I finally wised up after I went into the Air Force and quit the month I turned twenty-one. Oh, the irony!

Neither Terry nor Dick ever worked with me, picking berries or beans in our earlier years. I think they did pick for someone but not at the same places I worked until we were in our teens. Then Dick did work for Mr. Morris enough to get the job with me, weighing and irrigating beans.

Nancy Hackett lived next door from about halfway through grade school until after I left for the military. I guess at one point in growing up, I had a crush on her, but for the most part, she was always the girl next door, the one I could talk to and get the scoop from about other girls. We spent a lot of evenings sitting on the cement wall of the steps leading up to their front door, talking about everything and nothing at all, usually about all the other kids we knew. Joan, who lived down toward the canal from us, came to visit Nancy a lot, and we boys would stand in my backyard, talking to them through Nancy's upstairs bedroom window. Boys and girls hanging out together in a bedroom was not acceptable in those days.

Rick was the guy with the '49 Chevy coupe that we pushed almost as much as we rode in. He was, as I've said, a few years older, and he had a sister that was two years younger than we were. They lived on a side street between Terry and me. Linda was a wild child, quite spoiled, and used to getting whatever she wanted. Their dad owned a roofing company, so they had more money than the rest of us kids, and she loved to flaunt it! But in spite of it all, we were all good friends, and she was the only one that ever got away with calling me anything but Ed. She insisted on calling me Jonathan, although I never knew why. I think it was just because she knew she could.

After high school graduation, Dick joined the Air Force, and I never heard from him again. Terry didn't get to graduate with our class but did the following year, then he joined the Navy. But by then, I was in the Air Force too and didn't connect up with him again until our forty-year high school reunion.

My Cars and Working
at the Texaco Station

After I turned sixteen, I wanted to get my driver's license, as do all boys at that age. But Dad never let anyone drive his car, so Uncle Roy, in his usual generous style, let me use his '62 Dodge Dart to take the driving test. That was another day that will live in infamy. First of all, the DMV instructor I got was the ogre every kid dreaded. He had the personality of wallpaper and an attitude that would cool molten lava. So right off the bat, I was scared to death. In those days, you had to take the test in a car with a standard shift. My uncle's Dodge had a clutch with what they called a double-action spring. That meant a spring helped hold the pedal down when you pushed it to the floor, but halfway up, that same spring took over and assisted in lifting it up. Well, that spring was the death of me, and since my knees were already knocking, when I started to leave the DMV, I popped that clutch and peeled rubber right out of the parking lot! There went ten points off my grade right off. Then he told me to get in the right lane, so I did—right on the railroad track. That's a no-no, so there went another ten points. The third thing I got docked for, I always thought was wrong. When we turned back to Main Street, which was a one-way to my left, I waited for the traffic light to turn green then turned left. He took off another ten points because he said it was legal to turn left onto a one-way street on a red light after stopping, and I didn't. So I flunked the driving test the first time. If I had been thirty years old or so, I might have contested his ruling, but when you're sixteen and scared to death, his word is the gospel. Anyway, the second time I tried, I passed the test just fine and even got a compliment on my parallel parking, which I completed on the first try.

That summer after I was sixteen, I made enough money weighing and irrigating beans that I bought my first car, a pea-green '49 Ford with beautiful tuck-and-roll upholstery, which was THE THING to have back then. I bought it from a kid who had just moved down from Washington state for $100. What I didn't know was that he had moved down from the coast of Washington, and the body of that Ford was so rusted out. Some of it was about as thin as a Kleenex! The first time I took it out on one of our rubboard gravel roads, a big chunk of metal under the passenger door just fell right out. That's when I knew I'd been had.

I kind of left out part of the story about that first car. I had enough extra cash of my own, so I didn't bother to ask Dad if I could buy it, knowing I would just get a long lecture on why I shouldn't. As it turned out, I got the lecture anyway. He threw a real "hissy fit," asking me how I thought I could support a car once the summer work was over. After all, there was gas, tires, insurance, and some other things—I had stopped listening by then! I told him it was my decision, and I would work out a solution. And I did. I went next door and asked Dave for a job at his Texaco station. It just happened he needed someone, and he knew I was reliable. I continued to work for him for $1.25/hour until I graduated, working most weeknights until closing and usually Saturdays and Sundays—especially Sundays since Dave wanted the day off. And yes, I bought all my own gas, tires, insurance, and whatever those other things were that I couldn't remember.

I guess I should take a little side trip at this point and tell about my adventures working at the gas station. As I said, I worked for Dave from September 1963 until June 1965, when I graduated from high school, and a lot can happen in twenty-two months!

I got out of school a little after 3 p.m. and would go home, change into my Texaco uniform (yes, we wore the green pants and shirt with the Texaco star on the shirt!), grab something to eat, and head for the station. It was out on the I-5 freeway, about 8 miles from Lebanon, so I got there about four thirty and worked until closing on weeknights. In the dead of winter, when business got slower, I usually got off by 9:00 p.m. then would work Saturdays and Sundays as needed. Dave was Catholic, so he didn't like to work on Sunday; therefore, I'd open up at about 8:00 a.m. and work all day. He would show up occasionally in the afternoon for an hour or so just to see how business was going then go back home.

Weekdays during the winter, I worked a lot of nights alone, but on weekends and spring, summer, and fall, when it was busier, we had a couple of others who worked there. One guy was old Frank, a German guy about sixty years old (hey—that was "old" to me then!) who was a good employee but who moved like slow molasses, as they say. He drove a pea-green '55 Chevy that burned oil, so every time he poured a quart into a customer's car, he'd take the can into the back of the lube room and turn it upside down on another oil can, so the tablespoon or so in the can wasn't wasted. Talk about conservation—Frank wasted nothing! We didn't do any major car repairs at the station, but because it was on the freeway, we sold oil, batteries, and tires. And because a lot of the older cars back then did burn some oil, we sold a lot of it. When Frank managed to accumulate a half quart or so, he'd take it out and pour it into his car, so he never had to buy any!

The only other person who worked there during my career was Dave's nephew, Val. His dad was a teacher at Lebanon High School, who taught health and family living, but a lot of us behind his back called it sex and filthy living class. And to make even more mockery of the poor guy, his name was Al Newman—very close to the name Alfred E. Neuman, the main character in *Mad Magazine*, which was popular at the time. Anyway, all this to say that when Val first came there, my first impression of him was that he was very spoiled, the kind of kid that had never had to work for anything so far in his life. He came there the following summer after I did, right after school let out for the summer, and that was already a very busy time at a freeway station due to the tourist traffic. So early on, I was thinking, "I not only have to do my own work but also train Val to keep him moving and to make sure he doesn't screw up anything or short the till making change." The good news in all this is that after those months with his "feet to the fire," so to speak, Val turned out to be a good station attendant and continued to work some weekends after school started up again.

All during the summer, freeway traffic was pretty busy, so we would many times be open until midnight. Dave tried staying open twenty-four hours a day one time, but we found that the customer traffic died down too much in the wee hours of the night. One night pretty late, when I was alone (again!), a whole flock of cars came in on me all at once. They were traveling together and made a point of trying to confuse me with all different requests for the amounts of gas, what they wanted to be done under the hood, and anything else they could think of. What I didn't know until they were all gone was while I was running my rear off outside, their wives and kids were inside, taking all the gum and candy we sold on a rack by the cash register stand! Even at the prices then, they probably stole about $40 or $50 worth of merchandise from me. But Dave surprised me and didn't make me pay for it. He had seen them come in before and warned me that I would probably see them again sometime. They were a band of "gypsies" that went down to Los Angeles, bought used cars at a big auction there, and drove them to Portland to their used-car lots to sell. And sure enough, some months later, they came in again. That time I was wiser and locked the office door until I collected their money and went back in to make change.

One of the most valuable lessons I learned working at a service station is NEVER stick your hand into someone's car window to pet their dog. While washing a windshield one day, I noticed a tiny Chihuahua lying on the back of the driver's seat, where the headrest would be today. Since the window was open, I thought, "What a cute little dog," and reached in to pet his head. He just about took my hand off. No blood, mind you, but some severe lacerations on my hand. Dogs are very territorial about their cars!

Next door to the gas station was the Oregon Restaurant. The proprietor of that establishment was a guy named Shirley. Well, being young and new to the world, I thought that was a very strange name for a guy. After all, my sister-in-law, Bob's wife, was named Shirley! Of course, I made the mistake of kidding him about it one day while

I was enjoying a coffee break. Boy, was that a mistake! I spent the rest of my break being lectured about how, until Shirley Temple came along and messed things up, Shirley was a common name for men. Whether the lesson was true or not, it was one hard-learned!

Oh, and we must not forget the English couple that came in one day in their Mercedes. As they were heading for the restaurant, he told me to "fill it with petrol and check under the bonnet." I looked at Dave, and he started to laugh. He said just do what I always did—fill it with gas and check under the hood. Darn people! Why don't they speak English like we do? That was second place to the construction foreman that came in right after I started there with all three of his trucks. He hit the ground running for the restaurant and said to fill them all, check the oil and water, and change the air in the tires! Well, you can imagine my panic? Change the AIR in a dozen tires? And how was I supposed to do that? Dave to the rescue again— he said not to pay any attention to the guy, that he was just giving me a hard time because he knew I was new! After that first initiation, the guy turned out to be a good guy and a regular customer. After all, each of his trucks would take $7 or $8 worth of gas! At around 30¢ a gallon, that was a BIG sale.

One of the most memorable events for me during that few years was one Saturday night, just about closing time, a Cadillac sedan pulled in with about a half dozen guys in it, needing gas. Those guys turned out to be Paul Revere and the Raiders, a fairly new rock and roll group at the time (they're still performing, and you can still hear some of their hits on the oldies stations). They had just finished a show over in Albany at the National Guard Armory, a popular place for major events. But the thing I remember most was that after I had filled the car with gas, washed the windshield, and checked the oil (standard procedure back then), one of them walked to the back, opened the trunk, and paid me from a briefcase full of cash! I was never so shocked in my life—they must have been paid for their show in cash! I don't think I've seen quite that quantity of money in one place since then. And no, I don't even remember what they looked like. I was pretty busy, and they weren't dressed in the costumes they wore on stage anyway.

I think we tend to remember more negative events in our lives than positive, like our failures or embarrassments or moments of disfavor with others. I had one of the latter one Sunday morning when an older lady came driving in very slowly with one tire flat. While I put her flat tire on the mount and repaired it, she spent the whole time telling me how, were it not for the flat tire, she would be in church right now and how I should not be working on Sunday but should also be in church! Well, I was raised not to argue with my elders, plus back then, we were taught that the customer was always right, so I didn't point out to the lady that, were it not for me being there at that time, she would be sitting on the side of the road with no help!

As I mentioned, I worked at the gas station until I graduated in June 1965. I knew I needed a better job until I could go to college, so I managed to get the job at Linn Gear in July. I worked there until just before I went into the Air Force.

Now where was I? Oh yes, I had just purchased the pea-green '49 Ford for $100, much to the irritation of my dad. And I had just discovered that its body was all rusted out. All was not lost with the green pea, however, because there was another guy in town that had a tan '53 Ford that he wanted to trade me straight across. So we did. That '53 had been rolled once, but since cars in those days were like Sherman tanks compared to the metal in the ones now, only the top was damaged. I say "damaged," which is a nicer way to say it looked like someone had taken a giant meat cleaver to the top then tried to pop it back out with a hammer. Okay, so it was kind of ugly, but no windows were broken, and it ran great!

Only a few short months went by until I sold the '53 Ford. I got $350 for a car that I had $100 invested in. That was the good news. The bad news was that Dad, in his more elderly wisdom, had found a '56 Ford sedan down at one of the local used-car lots that he thought I should have—it was dependable—the word that strikes fear into the heart of any teenager! It had to be the last car anyone in their teens would ever choose since it was an ugly slate gray, had four doors, a sickly six-cylinder engine, and black-wall tires! But since I didn't have much cash, I couldn't be too choosey, so I bought it. I spent the next year hoping the thing would blow up so I could get rid of it.

Two unfortunate incidents came out of owning that ugly gray car. In the first one, a Lebanon cop pulled us over one Saturday night and told me I should follow him down to Ray Spiers' Chevron station by what we called the "Y" or where Park Street split off from Main Street. Well, we couldn't imagine why we should have to go there, but I did, knowing that Ray was a good friend of mine and my brothers—we bought a lot of our gas from him. When we got there and got out of the car, Ray came out, pretty indignant toward the cop, and told him in very short terms that he had described a SILVER Ford, not gray, and CHROME WHEELS, not chrome hubcaps, and that he had not recognized the occupants of the other car, whereas he knew us very well! So the chastised and slightly embarrassed cop turned us loose. We found out later from Ray that there had been a car matching that description in town from Albany, our neighbor about 10 miles away. The guys in it had torn up his restroom, tearing the towel dispenser off the wall and more. However, the cops never caught the culprits.

On another Friday or Saturday night, while we were dragging the gut, one of our local cops stopped us once again. He wanted to know if I had just come across from Park to Main on such and such a street. When I told him yes, he said he was going to cite me for "excessive noise with the tires." We had never heard of such a citation, but for just a moment or two, I really wanted to plead guilty— it would have been a real conversation piece next week in school or down at Ritchie's Drive-In! But my sanity quickly returned, and I laughed and assured the officer that the "sick-six" in my car would no way make any noise with the tires, no matter how much you revved it and popped the clutch. I finally had to demonstrate to prove it to him, and he let us go—again. I always had a feeling that the guy in the silver Ford had been visiting from Albany again! According to the word on the street, that guy had a pretty hot V-8 in his.

About a year after I bought the ugly gray thing, I got my wish. Even though I had tried to blow something up, it had withstood all my abuse and kept running. Then one evening, as I was taking Mary

Swanson and her sister Eunice home from Ritchie's, we had stopped partway down their gravel lane to talk to a guy from their church who was coming out. Their lane went straight off from the paved county road, whereas the county road made a square right turn. As we were sitting there, a guy driving a mid-'50s Cadillac, which really was a Sherman tank, apparently had "had a few" at the local tavern and missed the right turn. Down the lane, he came, crashing into the rear of my car at probably 40 mph or more. Fortunately, he swerved just enough that he hit my right rear corner with his left front, but he knocked us down the road about 50 feet or so, and he landed in the ditch. Since the lane was a somewhat private road, going only to a few houses, the driver was not cited, even though he had been drinking. Things were different back then. The miracle was that even though my car had no headrests at all, none of the three of us suffered any permanent whiplash! Of course, we all had sore necks for a few days, but it was unbelievable that no one was seriously hurt.

Not so lucky for my car, however. When I got it towed home and got a look at it in the daylight, the rear bumper was up about even with the back window, had there been any back window left. The trunk lid was folded up like a cheap wallet, and the back seat now had about the same legroom as a Geo Metro! Yep, it was pretty well totaled. I didn't know what I was going to do since the driver of the Cadillac had confessed that he had no insurance (another no-no in today's world!). But about two days later, I got my answer. The guy called me and asked if he could meet with me. I did, and he said that he was a "powder monkey" (explosives expert) on the Green Peter Dam project up in the foothills above Sweet Home. He made good money but hadn't bothered to spend any of it on insurance. He knew that any one of us three could end up with serious and permanent neck injuries, so he said if I would sign a paper releasing him from any liability, he would just pay me $500 cash! Well, I know now that it was a dumb thing to do, but all I heard was the "$500 cash" part, so I signed. The only saving feature of it all was that I was still a minor, and so the release form probably wasn't worth the paper it was written on. Anyway, there I was, rid of that ugly car and five hundred smackers burning a hole in my wallet. As a sidenote, I also sold the engine, seats, and some other parts of the wrecked car to a nice gentleman for an additional $100 then had the carcass towed to the wrecking yard.

Enter the car of my dreams—the '56 Chevy Bel-Air four-door hardtop! From the moment I spotted that car on a lot in Sweet Home, I knew it was meant for me. And whattaya know—they were asking $500 for it. Of course, that just convinced me even more that the car was supposed to be mine. I bought it. It was a metallic copper on the bottom with a snow-white top. And under the hood…you guessed it, a beautiful V-8 with triple carburetors! Well, for exactly thirteen days after I bought it, I was walking—or should I say driving—on air. Then the bad news came. As I was about a quarter mile from Hackett's Texaco one afternoon, going to work after school, I started hearing this ear-piercing screech. Smoke started coming from under the hood, then the engine just quit. Fortunately, I could put it out of gear and coast the rest of the way to the station. I couldn't imagine what could be wrong with my dream machine. I had to call my buddy Terry, who towed me home after work that night. Soon after, he and I, with a lot of help from a friend of his who worked with his dad at a machine shop, tore the engine down to find the damage and rebuild it. It turned out that the previous owner had put some wrong parts in around the crankshaft, and they had come loose and spun around the shaft, damaging it beyond repair. But with good help and quite a few of my bucks, we finally had my Chevy back on the road. I always loved that car and wished I had kept it through all these years, but it wasn't meant to be.

There was one car during my high school years that I would have given up the '56 Chevy for, but it was never mine. In the fall of 1963, Wayne was at home between his two tours in the Navy. He bought a brand-new 1964 Chevrolet Chevelle Malibu Super Sport right off the showroom floor. It was a deep forest green on the bottom and a silvery mint green on top. It had black vinyl bucket seats, chrome wheels, a 283 cubic inch V-8 engine, dual exhaust, and a four-speed floor shift—all for the grand sum of $3,800! Oh, how I loved that car! The next year, he reenlisted in the Navy, mainly because he had overextended his credit and let the dealer take the car back. I begged like a dog for him to let me take over the payments, which were a whopping $118 a month back then. But he was afraid I couldn't afford the payments, working at the Texaco station for $1.25 an hour. So the dealer took the car, sold it at auction, and socked Wayne another $1,000 for his so-called "loss." I'm just sure I would have managed the payments somehow!

It was in the late fall of 1964, while he still had the Chevelle SS, that Wayne met Mary Swanson's sister, Eunice. Since Mary was so young then, her father insisted that someone go with us after church on Sunday night if I wanted to take her for a Coke or whatever at Ritchie's. That "chaperone" was usually Eunice. So one Sunday night, we were all three at Ritchie's when Wayne drove in in his fancy new car. I introduced the girls to him, and apparently, he and Eunice continued to see each other for the few weeks following, just before he went back into the Navy. He put in his two years in Hawaii, during which time they corresponded by mail. He came home in December 1966 while I was home on leave from the Air Force, and they were married the next month. I often wished they had taken more time to get better acquainted, but that was not for me to say.

Then there was the trip we took to Portland to buy Terry a car. His uncle Bill knew we didn't know much about buying used cars, and we certainly didn't know our way around the shysters in Portland. So he agreed to drive us up there and help Terry pick out a good used vehicle. In those days, McDonald's didn't have a place on every corner like they do today. They had only expanded to the largest cities, so that was also our first experience with eating at one. As I recall, the small hamburgers were six for a dollar! Wow! We thought we were really uptown—going where none of us had gone before!

We did eventually, after visiting several used car lots, find a '57 Ford sedan that Uncle Bill thought was a good enough purchase. Terry has reminded me lately that he didn't drive it out of the city, as he was too afraid something would happen. So with his cousin driving, we were making our way across town when suddenly the engine started making this terrible knocking sound! Well, you can imagine, Terry immediately thought the worst—that his hard-earned dollars were going right down the ol' toilet. We pulled into the nearest service station (yes, they actually had "service" in those days), and Uncle Bill knew just what to do. He bought a can of Bardahl, which was a good gas additive that helped clean up the inside of your engine, and poured that into the tank with the engine running. In just a couple of minutes, the black smoke started rolling out the tailpipe looking like a house afire, but soon that abated, and the knocking stopped. What Bill knew was that the sound was just valve lifters sticking because the car had been sitting idle too long. That engine continued to run perfectly for a couple of years for Terry then another few years for Wayne. Terry sold the car to him because Terry was going into the Navy, and Wayne had just got out.

Since we're talking about cars, I feel that I must mention the '41 Chevy four-door sedan the three of us bought, intending to chop it down to make ourselves a dune buggy. Naturally, our ambitions far outweighed our budget and abilities, so the dune buggy never materialized, but we sure had some experiences trying. Like the day we decided someone should break out the windshield with this gigantic sledgehammer. Little did we know that tempered glass windshields are made to withstand almost anything! I got up on the top of the car and took my best shot with the hammer, only to have it bounce off the windshield and go flying back over my head, nearly ripping my arms off! It was a lot funnier after I realized that all my major body parts were still intact. We messed around with that old car for several months until we realized we didn't have the money to finish the job, so we sold what was left to a wrecking yard. But, of course, it was fun while it lasted.

I have mentioned somewhere in this story that I tried to work a year after graduation so I would have the money to go to college. I graduated in June 1965 and went to work at that same machine shop as everyone else, Linn Gear Works. But by December 1965, Uncle Sam sent me my draft notice for the Army, and I instead joined the Air Force with my entry date being the next April. I did not have a safe, dry place to store the Chevy while I was gone, so it would have had to just sit in my folks' backyard. Plus, there was, at least I thought at the time, the possibility that I would never come back. It was the middle of the Vietnam War, and I didn't know what part I would play in it. I didn't know then that I would never leave the fifty states! So I thought the best thing I could do at the time was selling my beautiful car to someone who would love it. I did, and the guy whom I thought would love it blew the rear-end out of it before he got out of sight of my house! He was trying to show off his hot new car, popped the clutch right after he hit the pavement on Russell Drive, and POW! There went the differential. But he got it repaired just as I had, and they lived happily ever after as far as I know.

Before I sold the '56, I had been running rear tires that we called "cheater slicks." Because racing slicks were not legal on the highway, they made ten-inch wide slicks with just two grooves in each, which made them legal—hence the name. But before I sold my friend the car, I took those tires off and replaced them with the original street tires. I knew those cheater slicks were in high demand, and they were still brand new. I was able to trade them to another guy I knew for a '56 Dodge two-door sedan that had been lowered in the front. Now the method they had used to lower the car made it look really cool, but what they had done was heat the front coil springs until they collapsed. Although it looked good, it rode like an 1850s buckboard! Oh well, I figured I didn't have too much invested in the car, and it ran very well, so it would do just fine until I had to leave for the military. Plus, it wasn't anything I couldn't leave in Dad's backyard. As it turned out, that Dodge was a pretty good car. It had a small V-8 engine and an automatic transmission, with push buttons on the dash to select gears. Because there was no spring action in the front end, it also cornered like a Ferrari! One night, after playing cards at Jim's house out in the country, I was coming in on the river road to town and decided to just see what it would do on all those curves. I guess it wasn't too wise of me, but I was taking the corners so fast that the rear end was drifting. Since it didn't lean, it held the road like I was in the Indy 500 (or so it seemed to me). What I didn't know until later was that Terry, my buddy, had driven out toward Jim's house looking for me, spotted me driving back, and had tried to keep up with me in his '57 Ford. Well, he said later that he gave up trying and thought I had lost my mind!

Just a few weeks before I left home, I blew the driveline on the Dodge and towed it to my dad's backyard, where it sat long after I left home. I was told that my brother Ray sold it for parts, but Ray said he didn't, so I guess Dad got rid of it somehow. Anyway, on April 15, 1966, I went to Portland and flew out to San Antonio, Texas, with a group of inductees for boot camp. That was the end of my life in a small lumber town in Oregon.

Epilogue

Almost fifty years later, in 2013, after living about forty years in California and seven years in Idaho, my wife and I moved back to Lebanon, my old hometown. It's not the same as before—the mills are mostly gone, and so the economy is not centered around the timber industry. And, of course, the town has changed— no Durlam's Bakery, no skating rink, no Dairy Queen. And our old Ritchie's Drive-In hamburger joint is now a small Mexican take-out restaurant. There are coffee kiosks on every corner. But by chance, we now live in the country just across the road from my oldest and best chum, Terry. And my only surviving brother Ray is just up the road from us. So all in all, it is good to be home again.

About the Author

John Leard was born in a small town in Texas, seventh of eight children, to a farming family. At the age of four, he moved with his family to the small lumber town of Lebanon, Oregon. Here, he grew up, working in the fields every summer, picking crops, then working through high school as a service station attendant. This book was initially his attempt to help his children understand what his life was like in those days. After graduation from high school, he spent four years in the Air Force during the Vietnam War as an airborne radio technician. He went on to work for the electric company as a telecommunication technician until retirement, after which he and his wife, Sharon, moved to Idaho. There, they enjoyed fishing, camping, and exploring on ATVs with their son's family but finally got tired of the winter and snow. So in 2013, after forty-seven years, he and Sharon moved back to his hometown in Lebanon, where they still enjoy boating and fishing.

CPSIA information can be obtained
at www.ICGtesting.com
Printed in the USA
BVHW070919060423
661866BV00003B/473